SMYTHE LIBRARY

Stamp this label with the date for return.
Contact the Librarian if you wish to renew this book.

14 MAY 2010		

This book is dedicated to the inspirational memory of
Wing Commander George C. Unwin
DSO DFM*, 1913–2006

Last of the Few

18 Battle of Britain Fighter Pilots Tell Their Extraordinary Stories

Dilip Sarkar
MBE FRHistS

AMBERLEY

First published 2010

Amberley Publishing Plc
Cirencester Road, Chalford,
Stroud, Gloucestershire, GL6 8PE

www.amberley-books.com

ISBN 978 1 84868 435 5

British Library Cataloguing in Publication Data.

A catalogue record for this book is available from
the British Library.

Typeset in 10pt on 12pt Sabon.
Typesetting by FONTHILLDESIGN.
Printed in the UK.

CONTENTS

GLOSSARY

AA	Anti-aircraft (fire)
AAF	Auxiliary Air Force
CFS	Central Flying School
CO	Commanding Officer
EFTS	Elementary Flying Training School
FAA	Fleet Air Arm
FGS	Fighter Gunnery School
FTS	Flying Training School
HP	Horse Power
IO	Intelligence Officer
ITW	Initial Training Wing
ORB	Operations Record Book
OTU	Operational Training Unit
RAFVR	Royal Air Force Volunteer Reserve
R/T	Radio Telephone
SFTS	Service Flying Training School
U/S	Unserviceable
WAAF	Women's Auxiliary Air Force
Bogey	Unidentified radar plot

Bandit	Confirmed hostile aircraft
Scramble	Emergency take-off
Vector	Course to be steered
Angels	Height measured in thousands of feet
Tally Ho	Enemy sighted, attacking now
Pancake	To land
Drink	The sea
Freie-hunt	German Fighter sweep
Kampfgeschwader	German bomber group, comprising three wings
Jagdgeschwader	German fighter group, comprising three wings
Geschwaderstabschwarm	German fighter or bomber group staff flight
Gruppe	A German wing of three squadrons
Gruppenkommandeur	Wing Commander
Hitlerjugend	Hitler Youth
Kommodore	Group Commander
Rotte	A pair of German fighters
Schwarm	Section of four German fighters
Staffel	A German squadron
Staffelkapitän	The leader of a German squadron
Stuka	German Ju 87 dive-bomber

INTRODUCTION

The Battle of Britain was won not by Malan, Stanford-Tuck and me, who got all the accolades. It was won by kids of 19 or 20, who maybe shot down nothing or just one before being killed themselves. They were the blokes who really won the Battle of Britain, make no mistake there. They were determined, by going off to fight and being prepared to die if necessary.

So said Group Captain Sir Douglas Bader, that legless airman made a household name through Paul Brickhill's bestselling yarn *Reach for the Sky*, made into a globally successful film of the same name. The point made by Sir Douglas, that the Battle of Britain was not won by 'aces' – pilots who shot down five or more enemy aircraft – but by the rank and file is absolutely right. Certainly there were individual pilots with substantial personal scores, but it was the collective effort that was important. Indeed, after the event Lord Dowding, Fighter Command's Commander-in-Chief during our 'Finest Hour', commented: 'Think not of the Battle of Britain being won by individuals, but by a team.' That team, of course, comprised not just pilots, but fitters, riggers, armourers, plotters, and even cooks and cleaners – all of whom contributed to keeping Fighter Command on 'top line'.

Battle of Britain pilot Peter Fox, a sergeant pilot of the RAF Volunteer Reserve, once modestly described himself and peers as 'also rans'. As Sir Douglas emphasized it was these 'also rans', in fact, who really won the Battle of Britain. Unfortunately their experience has been considered of lesser importance by both writers and publishers, and with the limelight dominated by the likes of Douglas Bader and Bob Stanford-Tuck, the 'blokes who really won the Battle of Britain' have lacked a platform from which to record and share their experiences. It is these men, however, not the famous aces, who both fascinate and inspire me personally, recognizing years ago that the recording of their memories was equally crucial to collating as comprehensive a record as possible of summer 1940. So, some twenty-five years ago, without any historical or journalistic training whatsoever, but armed with enormous enthusiasm, a tape recorder and notebook, I was determined to expand the footprint that the Few would leave behind. My intention was to record the memories of the 'also rans', including lesser known aces, actively seeking out the surviving Few, corresponding at length with those it was impractical to visit. Consequently over the years since a unique archive of memories and photographs has been compiled, from which source the seventeen chapters in this book have largely been drawn.

Early on during my project, one particular thing became clear: the Few would comfortably speak of humorous incidents, even the trauma of being shot down – but not of anything that showed them in any kind of heroic light; 'shooting a line' was strictly taboo. When once told that the debt owed to the Few remains immeasurable, Keith Lawrence, a fighter ace from New Zealand, remarked simply: 'Oh, I think that's a bit much.' It is hardly surprising, then, that very often interviewing such self-effacing individuals could accurately be likened to squeezing blood from a stone.

The pilots whose stories are told in this book represent a microcosm of Fighter Command in 1940. The reader will find regular, professional, airmen, auxiliaries and volunteer reservists; the reader will not find the stereotypical fighter pilot, however: no handlebar moustaches here. Four of the pilots featured were eighteen during the Battle of Britain, the oldest twenty-eight; their average age was twenty-two. Some were aces, most were not; Ken Wilkinson, for example, describes his service as a 'no score draw', given that although he made no kills in the war-torn air, neither was he shot down by the Luftwaffe. The collective experience of lesser-known aces and 'also rans' therefore exists between these two covers.

The RAF was formed on 1 April 1918, a service independent of both the army and navy. The Air Force Cadet College at Cranwell provided training for regular officers; staff officers were trained at the Air Force Staff College at Andover; the Central Flying School at Upavon produced service pilots, and the Technical Apprenticeship Training Scheme at Halton provided engineers. After the Great War, as the world disarmed, the RAF was vastly reduced. In 1925, though, the Auxiliary Air Force (AAF) was formed, with four squadrons, each raised on a territorial basis. The auxiliaries, identifiable through the brass 'A' worn on their lapels, were largely young men of means who already flew for pleasure. Throughout the week they worked in their civilian jobs – lawyers, farmers, stockbrokers – training with their squadrons at the weekend. After Adolf Hitler came to power in 1933, it became increasingly obvious that another war with Germany was a distinct possibility. Consequently the RAF benefited from the Air Expansion Scheme, which saw, albeit at the eleventh hour, the formation of the RAF Volunteer Reserve (VR) in 1936. Whereas the AAF was formed from Britain's social élite, those young men who learned to fly with the VR came from ordinary backgrounds: grammar school boys, not Etonians, with policemen, for example, as fathers, not titled aristocrats. When called up for full time service shortly before the outbreak of World War Two, VR pilots were posted to and absorbed by both regular and auxiliary squadrons. The pilots in this book, therefore, include professional airmen, and both amateur auxiliaries and reservists.

Many adventurous and patriotic young men from the Commonwealth worked their passages to England when it was obvious that war was inevitable. So it was, therefore, that in 1940 Fighter Command comprised not just British pilots but also Australians, New Zealanders, South Africans and Canadians. After the fall of France, pilots came too from the occupied lands – Czechs, Poles, Belgians, French and Dutch. From neutral America came eleven volunteers. All were welcome; as Dowding said: 'We needed them all.'

Between the wars, however, it was the bomber, not fighter, force that was given priority. It was believed, as politician Stanley Baldwin put it in 1932, that the 'bomber would always get through', and that the 'only defence is offence', through retaliatory bombing, or at least the threat of it. While acknowledging the aeroplane to be 'the most offensive weapon ever invented', the 'Father of the Royal

Air Force', Marshal of the RAF Sir Hugh Trenchard, explained in 1921 that it was 'a shockingly bad weapon for defence'. Indeed, Trenchard thought so little of fighters that he considered them necessary only to 'keep up the morale of your own people'. Little wonder, then, that during the 1920s and 30s the bomber force was expanded at the fighter force's expense. When Hitler became Chancellor of Germany and embarked upon rearmament, the RAF remained equipped with obsolete biplanes similar to those used in the Great War. Indeed, biplanes remained the mainstay when the British Prime Minister Neville Chamberlain flew to Munich during those days of crisis in 1938; had Britain gone to war then, the German Me 109, a fast and modern monoplane, would have rapidly achieved aerial supremacy.

Fortunately, in 1934 the Air Ministry issued a tender for two monoplane fighters, ultimately resulting in the Hawker Hurricane and Supermarine Spitfire. Both were powered by the Rolls-Royce Merlin engine and armed with eight .303 machine-guns. The Hurricane first flew in 1935, the Spitfire a year later. Being easier to construct, Hawker's fighter went into production first, reaching the squadrons from December 1937 onwards; the Spitfire, superior in performance but more complicated to build, was not operational until August 1938. During the Battle of Britain, there were, in fact, thirty-three squadrons of Hurricanes but only nineteen of Spitfires. The Hurricane, however, was no match for the German Me 109 fighter, and it is true to say that the Battle of Britain would not have been won had Fighter Command been solely equipped with the Hurricane. Had Fighter Command faced the Luftwaffe with just its nineteen Spitfire squadrons, though, the battle would also have been lost, so the Hurricane was clearly essential in

1940. Although the pilots featured in this book flew Spitfires and Hurricanes, these were not the only fighter types: Defiants and Blenheims also played their part, but nonetheless the lion's share of action went to those fighting in the more charismatic single-seater and single-engined types.

Many of the following accounts concern pilots from both 10 and 12 Groups, rather than just 11 Group, the latter which covered London and the south-east and bore the brunt of the enemy's assault. Consequently, and through featuring the 'also rans', my intention is to offer a slightly different angle on the Battle of Britain. Indeed, much fighting took place over the West Country and the south coast, particularly from Portland east to Southampton, and, in any case, squadrons from neighbouring 10 and 12 Groups were frequently called to reinforce the hard-pressed defenders of London. Again, therefore, the collective experience is reinforced.

For official purposes the Battle of Britain is deemed to have been fought between 10 July and 31 October 1940, and by 71 RAF fighter squadrons and other units involving a total of 2,927 aircrew; 544 lost their lives in action that fateful summer. One of the pilots featured in this book was killed in 1942 (by 1945, another 790 of the Few had lost their lives on active service); two of them became prisoners of war after the Battle of Britain, all of which indicates the uncertain future faced by wartime fighter pilots. Moreover, six of the 'Last of the Few' have died since I researched and wrote their stories, so, as time marches on, the Few get increasingly fewer.

The Battle of Britain ranks amongst the most decisive battles in world history. Unsurprisingly, the survivors, even after all these years, remember those days with mixed emotions; it is appropriate to give the last word here to one of the Few, William Walker:

> They were the most exhilarating days, but one lost so many friends and they were all so young. It is sad that the best pilots seemed to get killed whilst the 'ham's' like me survived.

Dilip Sarkar MBE FRHistS, Worcester, June 2009

I

PILOT OFFICER C.F. CURRANT: 605 SQUADRON, HURRICANE PILOT

Christopher Frederick Currant was born in Luton on 14 December 1911, and joined the RAF in 1936. In the service he was inevitably known as 'Bunny'. Bunny first flew Gauntlet biplanes with 46 Squadron in 1937, followed by Hurricanes with 151 during 1939. Commissioned in April 1940, Pilot Officer Currant, a regular officer, joined the Auxiliary 605 'County of Warwick' Squadron at Wick in Scotland. On 21 May 1940, 605's Hurricanes flew to Hawkinge, just inland of Folkestone – the closest RAF station to France. From there the Squadron flew daily patrols over France to supplement the hard-pressed squadrons of the Advanced Air Striking Force. In March 1991, Bunny reflected on those dramatic events:

On May 21st, 1940, the Squadron was ordered off from Wick to Hawkinge, to be directed on offensive patrols over Northern France as the German army attempted to over-run Dunkirk. I was ordered to patrol the Arras area with Flying Officer Hope as my Number Two. As we prepared to take off, Squadron Leader Teddy Donaldson, the CO of 151 Squadron, landed from a patrol over

France and was rather pessimistic about the outlook over there. From our airfield I could see smoke on the horizon over France and hear the rumble of bombs dropping in the distance. We took off, climbed away heading for the scene of the battle clearly visible as we flew south. At about 15,000 feet in the Arras vicinity I saw He 111s dropping bombs. Saw them explode along the road and in the woods as I opened the throttle and dived towards the Heinkels. Gunsight on, straps tight and locked firm as I raced in with a quarter deflection from behind the Heinkel. Got it well in the sight and opened fire. Saw hits on the port engine and fuselage. Smoke, steam and flames appeared and it banked left in a fairly steep dive. The next thing was extraordinary. I saw and heard no enemy fire striking my aircraft but suddenly there was silence as the engine seized, the propeller stopped. There it was in front of my nose – just a stationary airscrew. The cockpit filled with fumes hissing noisily. Steam and glycol, but no smoke. I opened the hood, undid my straps and climbed out on to the wing, intending to jump. I then did a very stupid thing: I changed my mind. My mind said 'I can put this thing down!' I climbed back in and glided down and with wheels up slid into a field. I had no time to do up my straps and as the Hurricane skidded rapidly to a sudden stop I hit the side of the cockpit with my nose and broke it (the nose!) and cut my face. I clambered out, looked up to see Flying Officer Hope circling round and fly off back to Hawkinge. I grabbed my maps, parachute and Sidcot flying suit and made my way to a farmhouse where the folk very kindly bathed my cuts and we conversed quite ineffectively in pidgin French and English. I was aware of them pointing eastwards and could easily distinguish amongst the gabble of French words 'Les salles Boches', which I took to mean the bloody Germans. So

I was eager to head north towards Calais hoping to catch a boat back to England. I walked a long way still carrying my parachute, maps and Sidcot. I was bloody hot. It was a warm, sunny day. Eventually I walked into a small French town. Found the town hall and an official, and begged for a car to take me to Calais. Miracle, he did, and we drove past miles and miles of civilians in carts, bicycles, lorries, prams, old folk, young folk, kids and hundreds of French soldiers all heading west. What a terrible depressing shambles. We made Calais and I went aboard and at 10 pm that evening was back in the Officers' Mess of RAF Station Hawkinge. Next day I found myself in Folkestone hospital where they put me to sleep and fixed my nose. Re-joined 605 Squadron about three weeks later at Drem near Edinburgh. I was to find myself in the same Folkestone hospital several years later having a German bullet removed from my skull.

During the subsequent Battle of Britain, 605 Squadron operated from Croydon, and during that time Bunny accounted for nine enemy aircraft destroyed, which made him officially an ace, and shared in the destruction of several more. On 8 October 1940, he was awarded a DFC, and a Bar a month later. With the death of 605's CO in action on 1 November Bunny took temporary command of the Squadron. In early 1941, Flying Officer Currant was rested as an instructor. His return to operations in August 1941 saw Bunny given command of 501 'County of Gloucester' Squadron at Ibsley in Hampshire. During that period the morale-boosting film about the Spitfire's designer, Reginald Mitchell, entitled *The First of the Few*, was made at that station. 501 and 118 Squadrons supplied the Spitfires for the film. The opening scene showed David Niven talking to a group of fighter pilots on 'an airfield somewhere in England'. Those involved really were Spitfire pilots, including Bunny Currant himself. In June 1942, he was promoted to wing commander (flying), leading the Ibsley Wing; the following month he received the DSO for his work with 501 Squadron.

Wing Commander Currant later commanded 122 Wing of the 2nd Tactical Air Force (TAF), based at Gravesend and comprising 19, 65 and 122 Squadrons flying first Spitfire Mk IXs and then Mustang IIIs. Officially Bunny's final score of enemy aircraft destroyed was fifteen, and he shared in the destruction of at least five others. He remained in the post-war RAF and eventually retired in 1959. In 1945, while reflecting on his time as a fighter pilot, Bunny wrote a number of poems, two of which are reproduced here. After each poem are Bunny's memories of those particular events, written in 1994.

Croydon – September 1940

Once again he took to the air, and Croydon was the base
To fight it out in fear and sweat so many times each day
To smell the burn of cordite flash, to see the flames of war
High above the fields of Kent the dive, the zoom, the soar.
Returning from a clash of foes one day he came across
A sight which burnt deep in his soul and never can be lost.
A pilot dangling from his chute towards the earth did drift
He circled round this friend or foe so hopelessly alone
To keep away whoever dared to fire on such a gift.
It was a useless gesture, though, as round and round he flew

He saw as in an awful dream first smoke and then flames spew,
Curl up his back as arms he waved and burn the cords of life
Snapping the body from the chute, snatching him from war's strife.
With sickening horror in his heart, he landed back at base.
He cried himself to sleep that night in thanks to God's good grace
That he was spared yet once again to live and fight this fight
Against the things he saw as black, for things he believed were
right.

At the time of this event the battle over London and south-east
England was in full flow. We were busy. Oh boy were we busy!
There had been reports from RAF pilots of being shot at as they
floated down in their parachutes by Me 109s. I was racing back to
Croydon having expended all my ammunition in a great big melee
of Heinkel and Dornier bombers, Me 109s, Me 110s, Hurricanes
and Spitfires. I had attacked a number of bombers from above,
from the side, from below and head-on. It was a frantic whirl
of in-fire-break-down or up-and-in again and again. And then
there was no ammunition, all gone, head for home like mad. As
I flew westwards south of London I came across this pilot in his
parachute, yellow Mae West prominent. Ours or theirs I could not
tell. I knew about the attacks by Me 109s and so flew round and
round to stop any swine from attacking this pilot. I was determined
that no bugger would get this lad. No-one did. They'd got him
already as he had almost certainly baled out of his plane on fire.
Clothing wet from petrol, embers glowing, fanned by the air as he
floated down. Yes I wept myself to sleep that night, who wouldn't?

Redhill – March 1942

Until in 1942, high over Northern France
They hoped to lure Germans up to try their skill and chance
They used some bombers as a bait to bring them closely in
The trap worked well and on they came black crosses set on wing,
And in the fight that filled the sky he found himself alone
With three Focke Wulfs upon his tail, their guns ablaze with lead.
As bullets smashed his instruments and one went in his head
He felt the warmth of blood and sweat run down his hair and neck
And down he dived in swifter plunge to get close to the deck
As down and down he hurtled on he looked back to his tail
To see the flash of German gun pour out their deadly hail.
The earth rushed up to put a stop to screaming howling dive
He bent in two and pulled her through to zoom up and survive.
He weaved and jerked in desperate thought and prayed to God aloud,
And looking back he saw the grim black crosses of the foe.
They let him be, to get back free to cross the Channel grey.
With fearful heart and sickly pain he headed west for home
He turned the tap on oxygen pack to breathe and hope and pray
That engine sound would keep him bound for distant friendly coast,
For pure white cliffs that always seemed like splendid welcome host,
For waves of green that nature's scene would turn to fields of hay,
For native soil which gave such joy in which to live and play.
It seemed an age ere pilot caged in Spitfire's lovely shape,
Saw chequered earth of his own birth in patterns down below
Revealing there the larger square where airfield's shape did show.
Throttling back with lowered flap he circled in a glide

Locking tight the shoulder straps that held him safe inside,

Fingers flipped selector switch and wheels dropped into place

As airfield hedge slid underneath and grass rode up in grace

To meet the final flattening out of aircraft's slowing pace.

But bullet-punctured rubber tyres caused wheels to bite in deep

And in a flash there came the crash of somersaulted heap.

All was silent save the hiss of liquid on hot metal,

Something which to weary nerves meant only deadly petrol

Spilling out from smothered wreck of Spitfire upside down

Holding taut the pilot caught who struggled like a clown,

Terrified that trapped inside he'd be flame's hungry meal

Before the crews who rushed to help could lift the wreckage clear.

But powerful arms with heave and strain gave him the room to move,

He crawled away and felt strong hands his elbows firmly steer

To guide him to a stretcher close, to speed him on his way

To hospital in Folkestone to wait and think. He lay,

With thoughts that death was near to hand, to ponder on his wound

Would he survive or would he die? He prayed and felt much moved

As white clad figures wheeled him in to operate and probe.

On table top so still he lay as needle pierced the flesh

And anaesthetic washed his mind from all its fears so fresh

From all the vivid coloured strains that bit into the soul,

From all the longings in his heart, for life and victory whole.

Here comes Folkestone Hospital for the second time in two years. The scenario was this. Air Chief Marshal Leigh-Mallory, then Commander-in-Chief of Fighter Command, decided to operate large numbers of Spitfire squadrons over Northern France daily for weeks and months. Using small sections of RAF bombers as bait for the Luftwaffe to be drawn into battle with the dozens of escorting Spitfires. I was leading 501 Squadron escorting six Boston light bombers at 22,000 feet. In the kerfuffle that followed I found myself alone with three FW 190s and in the fierce scrap that followed I found to my cost that the Spitfire Mk V was no match for those vastly superior fighters. However, I was only hit once. At the same moment as some of my instruments disappeared in dust one bullet entered my skull – and STUCK. It passed through the cockpit canopy, through my helmet and into my skull and stopped, or I would not be writing to you now 52 years later. I rolled over and opening the throttle wide dived vertically for the ground 22,000 feet below. As I dived I looked back to watch each FW 190 sit behind me and fire – the Germans always used a lot of incendiary bullets which could easily be seen. As the first one broke away the next one took up the attack and then the third one. Not a single bullet hit the aircraft. When I got to tree-top level and below, I kept turning violently left, then right, missing trees and buildings by inches. They gave up as I neared the French coast, formed into a vic formation of three and flew off inland. The poem tells the rest. Today I still have seven tiny bits of a German bullet inside my skull The hospital gave me the bullet which years later I threw away – clot! I am now 83 and have no right to be alive.

2

FLIGHT LIEUTENANT P.M. BROTHERS: 32/257 SQUADRONS, HURRICANE PILOT

Peter Malam Brothers was another early correspondent who became a friend. Born at Westerham in Kent on 30 September 1917, being a young man of means he learnt to fly privately at the age of sixteen. Commissioned into the RAF in 1936, later that year he received his flying brevet and joined 32 Squadron at Biggin Hill. By late 1938 he was a flight commander, a position Peter still occupied when war broke out. In May 1940, 32 Squadron fought in France, and Flight Lieutenant Brothers opened his account as a fighter pilot when he destroyed an Me 109 on 19 May.

Having survived the Battle of France and the opening shots of the Battle of Britain, Peter was transferred to command a flight in 257 Squadron at Debden on 9 September. There he served under Squadron Leader Bob Stanford Tuck, and continued his success against the enemy. On 13 September, he was awarded the DFC (a Bar followed in 1943, and a DSO in 1944).

After the Battle of Britain, Peter formed and commanded an Australian Spitfire squadron, 457, and later led the Wings at Tangmere, Exeter, Culmhead and Milfield. After the war, he left the RAF and joined the colonial service in Kenya for a couple of years prior to coming home and re-joining the air force. Following a number of important appointments and commands, and having been made a CBE, Peter retired as an Air Commodore.

An enduring personal memory of time spent in the company of the Few is when I was honoured to be the Battle of Britain Fighter Association's guest at the 1997 annual reunion dinner. Every year a Memorial Flight Spitfire from Coningsby provides a nostalgic display for these distinguished airmen over Bentley Priory, Fighter Command's headquarters in 1940. At the appointed time, we all awaited the Spitfire's arrival with growing anticipation. Throughout that time I stood chatting to Peter, until our conversation was lost in the roar of a Merlin! As ever, Squadron Leader Paul Day provided an excellent display, which brought smiles and applause all round.

Although an ace, it remains virtually impossible to persuade Peter Brothers to discuss his own august exploits. Instead, characteristically, he too preferred to pay tribute to the 'also rans':

It was inevitable, of course, that not all of the pilots who fought in the Battle of Britain achieved the mystic figure of five enemy aircraft shot down, thereby confirming 'ace' status. Indeed, these were the majority who played a valiant part and without whom the Battle of Britain could not have been won.

Generally speaking, these were the gallant youngsters who joined the RAFVR pre-war. When called up, by having already learned to fly, they were ready to convert to and gain some experience of the Hurricane or Spitfire, the aircraft that they were to operate in battle. Or they were the ones who joined in the outbreak of war and were rushed through flying training, followed by considerably less experience of the aircraft they were to fly in combat.

The remaining non-regular element were the members of the then Auxiliary Air Force, later becoming the 'Royal', the so-called 'weekend flyers' who had the advantage in most cases of already being equipped with Hurricanes and Spitfires, or other operational types.

Reflecting after the war on our losses during the Battle of Britain, I noted that in my squadron, 32 at Biggin Hill, of our pre-war pilots there were some who had been shot down and baled out unhurt, or burnt, or wounded, or both, but none were killed. Our losses were the new boys who never had the time or opportunity not only to learn or be taught the tricks of the trade, but also to know the performance advantages and limits of their aircraft and how to exploit them. Tragically, they paid the ultimate penalty for their inexperience.

An example springs to mind. Prior to the Battle of Britain, operating over France as a flight commander, I naturally took our latest 'new boy' under my wing to fly as my Number Two. Suddenly I had that feeling we all experience at some time that I was being watched. Glancing in my rear-view mirror I was startled to see, immediately behind me and between my Number Two and me, the biggest and fattest Me 109 – ever! As I instantly took evasive action his front end lit up as he fired. I escaped unscathed, he climbed and vanished as I was doing a tight turn, looking for my Number Two. There he was, good man, cutting the corner to get back into position, as I thought, until he opened fire –at me! Suggesting on the radio that his action was unpopular, as there were no other aircraft in sight we wended our way home. Not only had he not warned me of the 109's presence or fired at it, he had had an easy shot at me but missed! I dealt a blow to his jauntiness by removing him from operations for two days intensive gunnery training. Sadly it failed to help him survive.

As so much time has now elapsed since this country's last major war, and the key to victory provided by the Battle of Britain, I am constantly being surprised by the interest shown in it by people from all walks of life and from so many different countries throughout the world. The interest of historians and military men I can understand, but they are the few, not the many, whose demands for information seems insatiable. Fortunately there are books like this to provide not merely information but also fascinating reading.

3

SERGEANT R.C. NUTTER: 257 SQUADRON, HURRICANE PILOT

Reginald Charles Nutter was a Volunteer Reserve pilot, having joined in March 1939. Reg received his flying badge in April 1940:

Just as French resistance was collapsing, Sergeant Don Hulbert and myself were posted to 601, a Hurricane squadron at Tangmere. The unit had been knocked about in France, where it had spent some time prior to our departure. We were soon posted to 257 Squadron at Hendon, which was a newly formed squadron working up on Spitfires.

At Hendon we went through the usual reporting in procedure and met our new CO, Squadron Leader Bayne. I was assigned to 'A' Flight, which was commanded by Flight Lieutenant Hugh Beresford. Our Spitfires were arriving in twos and threes, and after a 10-minute flight check in a Miles Master with Beresford, I was authorised to make my first Spitfire flight.

The weather was very warm and I was warned by the groundcrew not to spend too long taxiing around or the aircraft would overheat. On take off I was very impressed by the power of the Merlin engine and the Spitfire's rapid climb. In the air I found it a beautiful aircraft to handle because it was so light on the controls. I was somewhat disconcerted when it became time to land, as Hendon looked like a small green postage stamp, completely surrounded by houses. However, I managed to make a very credible landing and, feeling quite proud of myself, took off and made another one.

Most of the pilots joining the Squadron had neither been on a fighter squadron or flown Spitfires before. As a result the next three weeks were spent familiarising ourselves with the Spitfire. In the first week of June, we learned that we would be re-equipped with Hawker Hurricanes and shortly afterwards this type of aircraft began arriving at Hendon. On June 14th, I made my first trip in a Hurricane and found it much heavier at the controls, far less responsive and somewhat slower than the Spitfire.

During the working up period, Don Hulbert and me were sent to RAF Uxbridge for a radio procedure course. This proved to be quite interesting as it had a two-fold purpose – to train pilots in R/T procedures and to train the Fighter Controllers who would later control us from Operations Rooms. Marked out on the playing fields was a large map of the British Isles and a part of Western Europe. We pilots were given tricycles, which had formerly been used to sell ice cream! In the box at the front was a TR9 radio, which, at the time, was standard aircraft equipment. We wore headphones and were surrounded by a set of blinker like boards, which restricted our vision. The driving chain and sprockets were arranged in such a way that when we pedalled 25 times the wheel moved round just once! Thus our speed across the maps matched the speed of fighter aircraft across the ground at normal throttle settings. Down in the stadium a complete Operations Room had been built. This was fully manned by trainee Controllers, WAAF Plotters etc. On top of the stadium was a spotter who passed our position, and the position of the person designated as the 'enemy', down to the Operations Room. The 'Controllers' could then vector us by radio to make interceptions. We both learned a lot from the course but found it somewhat difficult to sit down on our final return to the Squadron. Pedalling around in the hot sun in a serge uniform made one quite sore in a certain part of one's anatomy!

By the end of June, Squadron Leader Bayne had us all whipped into pretty good shape. We had done a good deal of formation flying, air-to-ground and air-to-air firing. Around the beginning of July, the Squadron moved to Northolt where we practised 'scrambling' from real dispersal points. The airfield was also big enough for us to practise dusk and night landings.

From my logbook it appears that the Squadron was declared fully operational on July 20th, 1940. At about this time a change of command occurred with Squadron Leader Harkness replacing Bayne. We spent a good deal of the rest of the month operating out of Hawkinge, near Folkestone, with a return to Northolt each evening.

Early in August three of our pilots, Pilot Officer the Hon. David Coke, Pilot Officer Carl Capon and myself, were chosen to perform VIP escort duties. My log shows a flight to Christchurch escorting an American VIP, and on August 7th & 8th we escorted the Prime Minister, Winston Churchill, who was a passenger in a De Havilland Flamingo piloted by Flight Lieutenant Blenner-Hassett. The route was Hendon to North Coates, Manby, Coltishall to Hendon. This trip remains vivid in my memory as the PM persuaded his pilot to do some very low flying, for his personal amusement, across the Wash!

During the first half of August, the Squadron also operated on a daily basis out of North Weald to provide escort to convoys proceeding up or down the East Coast. We also operated out of Tangmere on a daily basis to provide similar cover to shipping in the English Channel. On August 8th, whilst on a convoy patrol, the Squadron tried to intercept some bombers which were attacking a convoy, but we were jumped by enemy fighters. In this first major engagement we lost three pilots: Flight Lieutenant Hall, Flying Officer D'Arcy Irvine and Sergeant Smith. This loss, coupled with the recent and unpopular change of command, caused a sharp drop in morale.

On August 15th we moved to Debden. This airfield had only just been completed and was very modern. From here we operated out of Martlesham Heath on a daily basis. Again we carried out many convoy patrols but also intercepted some of the larger raids in the London area. Towards the end of the month, Debden was heavily bombed and put more or less out of action. We had to move to Martlesham until things were sorted. It was during this period that Pilot Officers Chomley and Maffett were killed.

September was a very busy month with the Squadron flying many sorties and getting involved in plenty of fighting. During this phase the Germans were putting up really large fleets of bombers with heavy fighter escorts. We suffered further casualties, including Flight Lieutenant Beresford, Flying Officer Mitchell and Pilot Officer Bonseigneur.

Hugh Beresford was replaced as commander of 'A' Flight by Flight Lieutenant Peter Brothers, who came to us from 32

Squadron. At this time Harkness was also replaced as Commanding Officer by Squadron Leader Robert Stanford Tuck. This turned out to be very good news. We found Tuck to be a charismatic leader and this, combined with his exceptional combat record, gave me great confidence. His style of leadership contrasted greatly with that of his predecessor. Squadron Leader Tuck would make suggestions to the Controller as to how we might be better placed to make an interception, whereas Harkness would merely follow all instructions without question. When Tuck took us over morale was low. Under his inspired leadership there was a tremendous improvement. In many ways Tuck was an individualist but he could also play as part of the team. He would always go out of his way to provide other pilots with sound advice.

On September 2nd, we were patrolling off North Foreland when I managed to get some good bursts at a 109 which had swung in front of me whilst attempting to attack the Squadron from the rear. He immediately dived, streaming coolant, but I lost sight of him in the thick haze. On September 3rd, whilst intercepting a force of bombers attacking North Weald, I stupidly allowed myself to watch the fall of bombs across the aerodrome, instead of watching my tail. I was promptly pounced upon by an Me 110. Although my Hurricane got quite badly shot up and leaked petrol all over me, and despite having received shrapnel wounds on my right side, I managed to make it safely back to Martlesham Heath.

On October 7th we moved to North Weald. The daylight raids by large bomber fleets had ceased by this time, but the night raids on London and other cities had already begun. During daylight the Germans began employing Me 109s and 110s as fighter-bombers. These were nuisance raids intended to keep the British defences at a constant state of alert and demoralise the civilian population by the constant sounding of air raid warning sirens. These sorties tended to be flown at very high altitudes and formations were mixed with fighters not carrying bombs. Intercepting them was tiring work because of the high altitude involved, as in those days we had no pressurised cabin or flying suit.

For me personally the Battle of Britain remains a vivid kaleidoscope of memories. I recall trying to warn Pilot Officer Capon that he was about to be attacked by an Me 109 but my radio was unserviceable; I remember The Hon David Coke returning from a battle over Portsmouth during which a German bullet had nicked him in the little finger of his throttle hand. Once I chased a lone Do 17 reconnaissance bomber in and out of the clouds along the south coast whilst listening to American jazz music coming over our Squadron's radio frequency. Vivid memories all.

One incident not mentioned by Reg is the stirring low-level raid on North Weald by II/LG 2's Me 109 fighter-bombers, escorted by Major Adolf Galland's JG 26. This perfectly executed surprise attack left nineteen RAF personnel dead and forty-two more wounded. Flight Lieutenant Peter Brothers:

We all dived under a table when the attack came in! My car, an open 3-litre Bentley, was parked outside and I was livid to discover that a near-miss bomb had filled it with soil, which took forever to clean out!

A dozen 109s hit the airfield from two sides, causing mayhem. Some Hurricanes were trying to get up, but as the warning had come so late, it was hopeless. A bomb exploded beneath Sergeant Girdwood's Hurricane, shortly after becoming unstuck. The aircraft crashed in flames just beyond the aerodrome's north-west perimeter, killing the pilot. Flight Lieutenant 'Cowboy' Blatchford managed to take off, as did Sergeant Nutter and the Polish Pilot Officer Franek Surma. A skirmish rapidly developed above the smoking airfield. Blatchford thrusted at a 109, but was himself hit hard in a head-on attack by Hauptmann Gerhard Schöpfel, Gruppenkommandeur of III/JG 26. Fortunately Blatchford managed to crash-land his damaged fighter back at base. Reg Nutter was also in the fight, and attacked Schöpfel from the beam, but without result.

Pilot Officer Surma had seen the bombs falling, as he was taxiing across the aerodrome and preparing to take off. A bomb exploded on his left-hand side, shaking his aircraft forcibly, although he managed to get safely airborne through the lethal shot and shell directed at him. Climbing rapidly to 3,000 feet, the gallant Pole was also attacked by Schöpfel. A cannon shell exploded in the Hurricane's cockpit and this was soon filled with white smoke. Out of control, the Hurricane plunged into a spiral dive. After a struggle, Surma safely baled out at 1,000 feet. According to the Squadron Intelligence Report, he made:

> a successful parachute descent, landing in a treetop near Matching. After quickly convincing a Home Guard that he was a Pole and not a German, he was given two complimentary whiskies and driven back to the aerodrome. He had lost both flying boots when jumping out of the plane, received a black eye but was otherwise unharmed.

The Germans, however, did not escape unscathed. Three of the North Weald raiders were brought down. One enemy pilot was killed when his aircraft crashed at Goldhanger in Essex, another was captured and the third baled out but died refusing medical help from his British captors.

It was the story of Franek Surma, in fact, that brought Reg Nutter and I into contact nearly twenty years ago. The story of Flying Officer Surma was the subject of my second book, *The Invisible Thread: A Spitfire's Tale* (Ramrod Publications, 1992). My interest was stimulated by the fact that Surma baled out of a 308 Squadron Spitfire, R6644, which consequently crashed near my (then) home in Malvern on 11 May 1941 (albeit twenty years before I was born). Having traced local eyewitnesses and starting to research the incident, I was moved to discover that the twenty-five-year old Surma had been shot down over the Channel on 8 November 1941, and remained 'Missing in Action'. Going on to trace numerous pilots who had not only flown R6644 but also with Surma himself, I was able to reconstruct the period, and in particular the air battle in which this decorated Polish fighter ace lost his life.

In 1987, our Malvern Spitfire Team excavated the crash site of R6644 at a public event organized to raise money for the RAFA's 'Wings Appeal'. Our guests of honour were Polish Battle of Britain veterans Squadron Leaders 'Ghandi' Drobinski DFC and Ludwik Martel, both of whom unveiled the cairn that we had built to Franek Surma's memory. Ultimately I traced Franek Surma's two surviving sisters in Poland, who were both astonished and extremely moved to learn of our efforts to ensure that their brother's memory would live on. In 1988, I received an equally moving letter from them, part of which I reproduce below; any further comment would be superfluous.

Through your letter you have aroused our memories and have shown how wonderful people can be. Many special thanks go to you and we will be praying for your success in life, prayers for a person who is now very dear to us. May God take care of you and the organisation that you have created. We are so happy that there is still someone to light a candle for Franek on All Souls' Day. We are also happy because the memorial erected to him serves as his grave, a symbol that he can see from heaven. We have always been worried because Franek has no known grave. Now we are all at peace, thanks to you and your friends.

4

SERGEANT J. STOKOE: 603 SQUADRON, SPITFIRE PILOT

During my research into Spitfire R6644, the aircraft safely abandoned by Pilot Officer Franek Surma near Malvern on 11 May 1941, I was able to identify many pilots who had also flown this machine, and record their stories. The Spitfire concerned was taken on charge by No. 5 OTU at Aston Down on 6 June 1940, remaining there until damaged in a landing accident on 4 July. Reading the list of young pilots posted to Aston Down for Spitfire training is like reading a roll call of the lost, however, for so many went on to perish either during the Battle of Britain or later in the war. Names including Richard Hillary, Ray Aeberhardt, Eddy Egan, Gerald Maffett, Colin Francis, Robert Dewey, Noel Agazarian, Peter Pease; the list goes ever on and on.

Among those who flew R6644 and survived was Jack Stokoe, from Berwick, East Lothian, who reported for duty at Aston Down on 10 June. With him were Colin Francis and Eddy Egan, both of whom were reported 'Missing in Action' in 1940, but lay undiscovered with the wreckage of their fighters until recovered by aviation archaeologists long after the war. In total, thirty-eight young pilots arrived for instruction with Sergeant Stokoe and his friends, and all were posted to operational fighter squadrons just thirteen days later. This gives some idea of the volume of pilots processed by the OTUs during 1940 in an effort to maintain Dowding's squadrons at full strength.

In 1992, aviation artist Mark Postlethwaite and I visited Jack Stokoe at home, in the wilds of north Kent, and there recorded the following interview:

Only a year before the Battle of Britain began, my contemporaries and I were pursuing our civilian careers whilst learning to fly with the RAF VR in our spare time. The majority of us were 18-19 years old. Being aircrew, when called up in September 1939, we were automatically given the rank of sergeant, which at first caused some dismay amongst the ranks of professional sergeants, many of whom had taken 20 years to reach that exulted rank!

Most of us had only 50–60 hours flying on elementary types like Tiger Moths and Magisters when we were called up. After a brief spell at ITW to instil some discipline into us, we had about 100 hours on Harvards at FTS, which included a few trips actually firing guns. We were then posted to an OTU, in my case Aston Down, before being posted to an operational fighter squadron with just 10–15 hours on Spitfires recorded in our logbooks.

After training I was posted to 263 Squadron, which had first flown Gladiators, then Hurricanes, and was now converting to twin-engined Westland Whirlwinds. I chose to remain on singles, however, and so was posted to 603 'City of Edinburgh' Squadron, based at Dyce in Scotland. There were only three of us NCO pilots, the rest being officers, mostly auxiliaries.

By August 27th, 1940, we had moved to Hornchurch, just north of the Thames Estuary, by which time I had about 70 hours on

Spits and was therefore most fortunate. I could have gone straight to a front line fighter squadron from OTU, as indeed so many pilots did, and if so I would not have rated my chances of survival very highly. I had even already seen, but not actually engaged, two German reconnaissance bombers over northern Scotland.

On August 29th, we flew four patrols, intercepting Me 109s on two of them. I claimed one damaged but the trimming wires of my own aircraft were shot away. The following day we made four more interceptions, during the course of which I was credited with having destroyed an Me 109 and damaged another. Again, however, my own aircraft was damaged, by a cannon-shell in the windscreen, and my hand was slightly cut by splinters. On September 1st came three more interceptions of 20 plus bandits, one of which I shot down in flames over Canterbury.

On September 2nd, I was involved with two more interceptions, during the course of which I damaged two enemy aircraft but was myself shot down in flames, fortunately baling out. On that occasion, as I was attacking an enemy aircraft I remember machine-gun bullets, or maybe cannon shells, hitting my Spitfire, followed by flames in the cockpit as the petrol tanks exploded. I thought 'Christ! I've got to get out of here and *quick*!' I undid the straps and opened the hood, but this turned the flames into a blowtorch. I was not wearing gloves, as during our hasty scramble I had forgotten them, but had to put my hands back into the fire to invert the Spitfire so that I could drop out (no ejector seats in those days!). I remember seeing sheets of skin peeling off the backs of my hands before I fell out of the aeroplane. I was then concerned regarding whether the parachute would function or whether it had been damaged by fire, but I pulled the ripcord and fortunately it opened perfectly.

I landed in a field, but the Home Guard queried whether I was an enemy agent! A few choice words in English soon convinced them I was genuine, and thereafter I was rushed into the emergency hospital at Leeds Castle, suffering from shock and severe burns to my hands, neck and face.

I was in hospital for six weeks before returning to operational duties on October 22nd, with further combat successes. A second tour of duty with 54 Squadron followed, which included a second bale out (over the sea!). I was then seconded to a training unit but returned to ops, flying fighters, later in the war.

The point about the incident when I was shot down over Kent on September 2nd, 1940 is that at the time 603 Squadron was suffering such heavy casualties that that administration got pretty chaotic. For four days after baling out, although quite safe in hospital, I was officially posted 'Missing in Action'!

During the war, Jack destroyed a total of seven German aircraft and was awarded the DFC. Retiring from the service as a Squadron Leader in 1946, in 'civvy street' he became a trading standards officer. We attended a number of events in south-east England together, including the Biggin Hill air show in 2000, at which Jack was able to meet German Battle of Britain veteran and author Ulrich Steinhilper. Sadly, Jack died soon afterwards, and so passed another one-time courageous and dedicated pilot who had fought for his country during its hour of greatest need.

5

PILOT OFFICER G.H.E. WELFORD: 607 SQUADRON, HURRICANE PILOT

Harry Welford, in contrast to the majority of other pilots featured in this book, was a pre-war auxiliary member of 607 'County of Durham' Squadron. The following account, from Air Vice-Marshal Johnnie Johnson indicates the importance of social standing to the auxiliaries:

> I went along for this interview with the senior officer there (in 1938, with a view to joining the Auxiliary Air Force), who, knowing that I came from Leicestershire said: 'With whom do you hunt, Johnson?'
>
> I said: 'Hunt, Sir?'
>
> He said: 'Yes, Johnson, hunt. With whom do you hunt?'
>
> I said: 'Well I don't hunt, Sir, I shoot.'
>
> He said: 'Oh! Well thank you then, Johnson, that will be all!'
>
> Clearly the fact that I could shoot game on the wing impressed him not one bit. Had I been socially acceptable, however, by hunting with lord-so-and-so, things would have been different, but back then that is what the auxiliaries were like, and do not forget that many members were of independent means, which I certainly wasn't!

Johnnie, who went on to become the RAF's top scoring fighter pilot of WW2, still keen to do his bit, instead joined firstly the Leicestershire Yeomanry, a Territorial Army unit, and then the RAFVR. The rest, as they say, is history (see *Johnnie Johnson, Spitfire Top Gun, Part One*, Ramrod, 2002, and *Part Two*, Victory Books 2005, also by this author).

Harry Welford, however, describes how he came to be an auxiliary airman:

During 1939, my cousin Robert got permission to take me up to the Auxiliary Air Force base at Usworth and give me a 'flip', parlance for 'flying experience'. It was a fine day and ideal to get the feeling of 'no longer being earthbound', as my cousin put it. However, I knew that what goes up must come down again, so I was nervous. I was strapped in the front cockpit of an Avro dual control trainer with Robert in the rear. This seemed odd to me as I had expected the passenger to sit behind. Anyway we taxied out and Robert spoke to me through the intercom, swung into wind and took off. After a circuit of the airfield we did a trip over the local countryside pointing out such landmarks as Penshaw Monument, the River Wear, and, of course, Sunderland and Newcastle further north. All of these sights will remain in my memory as pointers to the aerodrome itself. My cousin asked how I liked it and my response was enthusiastic, whereupon he suggested performing the odd aerobatic. Before I could respond he dived steeply and performed a loop followed by a slow roll. My stomach was not feeling so good and I was quietly sick over the side. Robert must have seen my distress because he went down to land, by which time I was all right again. We joked about it but one of the senior officers must have spotted the mess in the cockpit and gave poor Robert a ticking off for doing aerobatics during an air experience exercise. He then made Robert clean up the cockpit.

Robert's aerobatics did not put Harry off, however, for on his twenty-second birthday, 4 December 1938, he was accepted for training with 607 'County of Durham' Squadron. Harry continues:

The Squadron's annual summer camp in 1939 was actually a prelude to war. None of us would be out of uniform for the next six years. Many would not survive for one year, let alone six. The summer camp concerned was at Abbotsinch, near Glasgow, which was the home base of 602 Squadron, another Auxiliary unit which was holding summer camp elsewhere. We pilots flew our machines up there whilst the ground crews were transported by road in advance of our arrival, erecting tents and marquees for servicing and messing facilities. The Gladiators took off in squadron formation and were a sight to be proud of, whilst we trainees followed in our Avro Tutors, in open order, led by the instructors. I was very proud to be flying solo on the longest cross-country I had done, although I was following the leading instructors and just wished that some of my fancied girlfriends could see me now!

In May 1939, I was commissioned into the Auxiliary Air Force as a Pilot Officer, and called to full-time service on August 24th. In October I completed my Service Flying Training and then went to 6 OTU at Sutton Bridge to learn how to fly Hurricanes. There we became familiar with all aspects of our Hurricanes and concentrated on aerobatics and more unconventional versions of them to avoid enemy attacks. We also did a lot of formation and simulated attacks and fighter tactics. A favourite exercise was to go up in pairs with an experienced pilot and then he would tell you over the R/T to follow him in all the manoeuvres he carried out. He aimed to lose you, and generally did, then got on your tail and the situation was reversed. Afterwards you discussed the different tactics of defence and attack, and the instructor would then advise you according to his experience.

Harry continues, describing his first encounter with the Hawker Hurricane:

Having previously only flown biplanes with fixed-pitch airscrews and no flaps, I required instruction on these additional facilities. I was therefore given dual instruction in a Harvard aircraft, which had most of the Hurricane's refinements, but not all, and no where near the power of its 1,280-HP Rolls-Royce Merlin engine. It was in the air when I started worrying how, in the name of heaven, I was going to get this thing called a Hurricane down again. I did a few manoeuvres and a couple of circuits, got my wheels and flaps down, my God how the speed dropped and how the attitude changed! I was coming down too steeply, I opened the throttle and she assumed a more gentle engine-assisted approach. I touched down and throttled back but then realised that I had not got much more aerodrome to pull up in. Hell, I was on the ground and intended to stay there. It being a grass airfield, I did not roll too far but far enough even with judicious braking to be just short of chopping the far hedge with my propeller. Nobody worried very much because I was sent off formation flying for the very next trip the same day.

At 1230 hours on August 15th, we were going off duty for 24 hours leave when the whole squadron was called to Readiness. We heard from the Group Operations Room that there was a big 'flap' on, that is a warning of imminent enemy action along the NE coast. We waited out at dispersal points, at 'Flights', for half an hour, then scrambled in squadron formation. I was in a feverish state of excitement and quickly took off and climbed up to our operational height of 20,000 feet ready to patrol the coast. We kept receiving messages over the R/T of 40 or 50 plus 'Bogeys' approaching Newcastle from the north. Although we patrolled for over half an hour, we never saw a thing. Just as I was expecting the order to 'Pancake', I heard the senior flight commander shout 'Tally Ho!', and 'Tally Ho' it was! There, on our port side at 9,000 feet must have been 120 bombers, all with swastikas and German crosses as large as life, having the gross impertinence to cruise down Northumberland and Durham's NE coast. These were the people who were going to bomb Newcastle and Sunderland where our families and friends lived, 607 Squadron being an Auxiliary unit raised from the local area.

I'd never seen anything like it. They were in two groups, one of about 70 and the other about 40, like two swarms of bees. There was no time to wait and we took up position and delivered No 3 attacks in sections. As only three machines at a time, in formation, attacked a line of 20 bombers, I just couldn't see how their gunners could miss us. We executed our attack, however, and despite the fact that I thought it was me being hit all over the place, it was their machines that started dropping out of the sky. In my excitement, during the next attack I only narrowly missed one of our own machines whilst doing a 'split arse' breakaway – there couldn't have been more than two feet between us! Eventually, spotting most of the enemy aircraft dropping down with only their undercarriages damaged, I chased a Heinkel and filled that poor devil with lead until first one, then the other engine stopped. I then enjoyed the sadistic satisfaction of watching the bomber crash into the sea. With the one I reckoned to have damaged during our first attack, these were my first bloods, and so I was naturally elated. The squadron suffered no losses, but claimed six He 111s and two Do 17s destroyed, five He 111s and one Do 17 probably destroyed, and four He 111s and one Do 17 damaged, although we now know that in fact, there were no Do 17s amongst the German formation.

I shall always remember September 8th, 1940, because this was the day after the evening that Betty Elise and I became engaged, but our move to Tangmere, in 11 Group, was confirmed that day. We were to relieve 43 Squadron whose CO, 'Tubby' Badger, had been shot down earlier in September and since which time the Squadron had been led by Flight Lieutenant Tom Morgan. Now, barely half the original complement of pilots were capable of operational duties.

Of course it was a tragedy so far as Betty was concerned but, though I felt the same, there was a war to be fought and we were trained fighter pilots. This was the beginning of the end, and as we all climbed into our Hurricanes having bid our 'adieus' that fine September day, I wondered how many of us would see Usworth or Newcastle again. Strange as it may seem, dirty, smoky, old Newcastle was to us seventh heaven when compared with the rolling green fields of southern England.

We arrived, however, at a completely blitzed aerodrome where we were greeted by the remnants of 43 Squadron: some on crutches, others with an arm in a sling, and yet another, who had had his face torn apart by an exploding cannon shell, with a head swathed in bandages. Though they had suffered so many casualties it was quite amazing to see them walking about. Needless to say they were very pleased to see us, having just been up on the third sortie that day and were still waiting for news of the latest casualties.

We only had time to re-fuel when we were called out on an operational trip that evening. There was no interception, however, and no casualties. The next morning, to my great disappointment, I was not called upon to fly and later the Squadron went off. In the event I was the more fortunate, as of twelve Hurricanes six were shot down. Three officers were killed and three sergeants wounded. Amongst the casualties were Stuart Parnall, my best friend, Scotty and the young South African George Drake. They were all lovely people, just like Alex Obelenski and 'Ching' Mackenzie, with whom I would have flown to hell, if necessary, in glorious comradeship.

With little experience, 607 Squadron had arrived at one of the 'hottest' sector stations at an extremely busy time. Without time to adjust to or train for the new operational conditions, it was inevitable that the lethal 109s would harshly treat the 'County of Durham' Hurricanes. Yet again, this RAF squadron, new to the fray, went on patrol flying a useless formation, and paid the price. As ever, the 109s had the advantage of height, sun, and used the excellent schwarm tactical formation. This divided each staffel into three sections of four aircraft that flew in line abreast, but the aircraft were well spread out so that there was no fear of collision. In the event of combat, the schwarm would split into two fighting pairs of leader and wingman, the rotte, so the fundamental principals were both flexibility and mutual support. It would not be until the 1941 'season' that Fighter Command grasped the benefits of and copied this enemy tactic. Harry goes on:

> Somehow we could not believe it. No one talked about it and we all hoped for news to filter through from some remote pub or perhaps a hospital. No news came, so we hardened ourselves to the worst: 'Killed in Action'. We bit back our tears and our sorrow. It was 'You heard about Stuart and Scotty? Rotten luck, wasn't it?' Someone would add 'And young George, bloody good blokes all of them'. After that epitaph the matter would be dismissed with the ordering of another round of drinks to avoid any trace of further sentiment.

Another problem faced by the auxiliaries was that losses did, in fact, affect personnel deeply given that these units were all locally raised. As a result, old school and family friends, business associates, even relatives, all served together. Casualties understandably had a depressing effect on these units.

By 17 September, twenty-three-year-old Pilot Officer Harry Welford was a veteran. On that day 'B' Flight scrambled at 1505 hours on the Squadron's fourth sortie of the day, Harry flying Blue 2. On this occasion the six Hurricanes patrolled the Biggin Hill/Gravesend line at 17,000 feet. Between 1500 and 1600 hours, a multi-wave massed enemy fighter sweep crossed the south coast. Each wave comprised two gruppen of 109s (some sixty fighters). Suddenly, 'B' Flight was bounced from above and behind by a horde of 109s:

When attacked we were warned to break formation. I broke and took evasive action, as a result of which I lost the Squadron. As we had instructions to re-form rather than fly alone, I saw a large group of fighters ahead, which I then intended to join up with until I realised that they were Me 109s! I fired a quick burst at them, but an unseen 109 fired at me and hit by air intake with a cannon shell. I did a quick flick roll that dropped me below cloud. No 109s about but a lone Hurricane that guarded my tail as I forced landed. The engine had seized and looking down I saw a field in which I thought I could land. As I approached, glycol and smoke streamed from the engine. When I opened the hood, these fumes were sucked through the cockpit and impaired my vision. The field was actually smaller than I thought, but there was a wattle fence that acted like a carrier's arrester hook. The plane then skidded across the second field but was brought to an abrupt halt by a tree at the far end, cracking my head on the reflector sight. Blood poured down my face, and thinking that the plane might catch fire I undid my straps and jumped out, only to fall flat on my face because my leg, which had been wounded by shrapnel, collapsed on me. Two farm workers rushed over and picked me up, putting me on a section of wattle fence. They told me that there was a German plane in the next field with the pilot in it, very dead. I regret now that I declined their offer to show me, but at the time I felt pretty dicky.

In hospital I gave my report to our flight commander, Flight Lieutenant Jim Bazin who acknowledged that I had shot down the 109 in the field next to where my Hurricane crashed. Now, however, I am not so sure as we have not been able to identity a potential candidate from the German crashes that day. Anyway, I was thereafter in hospital for a while with 'Tubby' Badger, 43 Squadron's former CO, who was very brave, always laughing. Sadly, he ultimately succumbed to his wounds, which was a great shame, as he was a fine man.

Research into this combat suggests that Harry was shot down by Hauptmann Eduard Neumann, Gruppenkommandeur of I/JG 27. The German's logbook confirms that he shot down two Hurricanes during this action, the other probably being 607 Squadron's Sergeant Landesdell, who was killed. Neumann was very experienced, having fought in the Spanish Civil War, and later became Kommodore of JG 27, which went to North Africa in 1941. There one of Neumann's pilots became one of the most incredibly successful fighter pilots of all time: Hans-Joachim Marseille, the 'Star of Africa'. Ultimately, Neumann's personal victory tally was thirteen, and he later became leader of the German fighter forces in Italy.

Both Harry Welford and Eduard Neumann survived the war. The former re-joined 607 Squadron on 20 October 1940, by which time the unit had been withdrawn to Turnhouse, in Scotland. During the Battle of Britain, 607 Squadron had lost nine pilots killed. For the next two months, Harry passed on his combat experience to replacement pilots before being posted away to be an instructor. He would not return to operations until November 1944, flying Spitfire Mk IXs with 222 Squadron and by which time the air war had changed significantly.

Soon after the war, Squadron Leader Harry Welford left the service, and at the time of our first contact, back in the mid-1980s, was living in comfortable retirement, with his Betty, on the Devonshire coast. We enjoyed voluminous correspondence and several meetings before Harry's passing in 1996; sadly, as time marches ever on, the Few get fewer.

6

SQUADRON LEADER B.J.E. LANE: 19 SQUADRON, SPITFIRE PILOT

As a child, fascinated by the Spitfire and Battle of Britain story, there was a particular photograph, repeated in numerous books and articles, that fascinated me. It showed a young squadron leader debriefing with other pilots and an intelligence officer. The pilots had just landed, and the squadron leader looked exhausted. I found it frustrating, however, that inevitably captions failed to identify the personalities concerned, generic captions reading simply 'Spitfire pilots after a sortie', or something similar. The face of the young squadron leader, lined and tired, haunted me, however, and I often wondered who he was and what became of him.

Many years later, I was given a book called *Spitfire! The Experiences of a Fighter Pilot*, by 'Squadron Leader B.J. Ellan'. The book was a first hand account published in 1942, and from the photographs within I was delighted to discover that this was actually the anonymous squadron leader whose photograph had captured my imagination so many years before. Subsequently I learned that his name was actually Brian John Edward Lane, CO of 19 Squadron in the Duxford Sector. Brian's book. *Spitfire!* was both an excellent and inspiring read, the author succeeding in answering 'the question of the man in the street: "What is it like up there?" and to give an idea of what a fighter pilot feels and thinks as he fights up there in the blue'. Having read the book, my impression was of an intelligent, brave but incredibly modest young man – an absolutely model human being. Among the pilots in this book, Brian Lane is unique, given that he perished during the war and has not, therefore, been interviewed personally for this book. Nonetheless, the first-hand account left behind in *Spitfire!*, coupled with the extensive notes in his flying logbook, preserved at the National Archive, provide the basis of this story. It is his surviving pilots, however – all of whom were interviewed – who provide the crucial memories around which this story revolves.

Brian Lane was born on 18 June 1917, in his words 'with a silver spoon in my mouth'. His family lived in Pinner, Middlesex, and Brian was educated at St Paul's, near Hammersmith Bridge. The school boasts some extremely distinguished old scholars, including the poet John Milton, the great diarist Samuel Pepys and, more recently, Field Marshal Lord Montgomery of Alamein. Unusually, therefore, for someone who had enjoyed the benefits of being educated at such a school, by 1935 the eighteen-year-old Brian was employed by 'a big electrical firm' and supervising a 'a dozen or so girls turning out hundreds of light bulbs'. Although the teenager considered his position to be a responsible one, in which he learned much about human nature, and women in particular, he was apparently not surprised when:

one day the powers that be informed me that the period of my employment coincided with a decline in their profits, and that if I would kindly leave them they could get along better without me. I went home to my lamenting parents with the additional news that I wanted to try for the RAF, which was then in the course of expansion.

Brian then applied for a Short Service Commission, and volunteered for pilot training, eventually being invited to a Selection Board at Adastral House. Feeling much like a 'microbe on a slide under a microscope' throughout the interview, Brian was successful and subsequently reported for duty at Air Service Training, Hamble, on 22 March 1936. There he completed *ab initio* flying training before moving on to No. 11 SFTS at Wittering on 3 June. Pilot Officer John Wray joined the service with Pilot Officer Lane:

Brian was rather languid and slow in those days, not what one imagined a fighter pilot to be. He was always known as 'Dopey' because he had deep set eyes with black rings underneath, nothing to do with his lifestyle, just natural characteristics! During those now far off days of our training, only the very good pilots went on to fighter squadrons, which meant, of course, the minority. For example, I was posted to an army co-operation squadron because, so I was told by the Chief Ground Instructor, 'they need gentlemen because you may have to take port with the general!

Upon conclusion of our course at Wittering, 'Dopey' was posted to a fighter squadron. I saw him afterwards on a number of occasions when he was with 19 Squadron at Duxford, and ran into him on other stations when his squadron was re-fuelling at forward bases such as Manston. In conclusion I must make one point absolutely clear: 'Dopey' Lane was no dope when it came to leading a fighter squadron.

On 8 January 1937, Pilot Officer Lane reported for flying duties with 66 Squadron at RAF Duxford, and flew the Gloster Gauntlet biplane fighter. On 30 June, Brian was posted to 213 Squadron, another Gauntlet squadron, based at Northolt, remaining with the unit until it was re-equipped with Hurricanes in 1939. On 11 November 1938, Brian was the pilot of a Miles Magister, in which his friend Pilot Officer Weatherill was a passenger, flying from Wittering to Northolt. The two pilots were going on leave for the weekend, but 3,000 feet over Henlow the aircraft went into a diving turn from which the pilot was unable to recover. In his log book, Brian wrote: 'Hit the deck at 12.50 hours at 200 m.p.h. Walked away from it – just. Returned to duty 3.1.39. longest weekend on record!' Not withstanding Brian Lane's amusing notes, the two pilots were lucky to survive. Brian was carrying his silver cigarette case, engraved 'BJL', the bottom of which sustained an 'L' shape dent in the crash. Across the damage, the owner has inscribed '11/11/38. Magister LS136'.

A week after Britain and France declared war on Nazi Germany on 3 September 1939, Brian was promoted to Flight Lieutenant and sent to command 19 Squadron's 'A' Flight at Duxford. 19 was a very famous squadron, not least because it was the first to receive Spitfires, on 4 August 1938. Pilot Officer Frank Brinsden was a New Zealander serving with the RAF, and recalls Flight Lieutenant Lane's arrival:

He was received politely but coolly as 'Sandy' Lane. Coolly because the residents of 19 Squadron thought that a number of them could have filled the vacancy without calling in an outsider who, despite the small number of officer pilots in Fighter Command at that time, was unknown to us. However, within a week or two Brian's calmness, personal dignity and professional skill showed through; the sobriquet 'Sandy' was never used again; within the Squadron he became simply 'Brian'.

The somewhat derogatory tag of 'Sandy' was quite incongruous. His dignity was not a pose and he enjoyed Squadron sorties to the local as much of any of us; he treated us all as equals. I do recall, however, a formal dressing down that I received from Brian Lane, after which my respect for him was even further enhanced; I used the same technique myself in later years, when a CO and with comparable results.

Pilot Officer Michael Lyne remembers the flying undertaken by 19 Squadron at this time:

I arrived on the Squadron fresh from Cranwell in August 1939. Brian Lane was my second flight commander and I found him to be a charming and encouraging superior. Our aircraft were Spitfire Mk I with fixed pitch two bladed wooden airscrews. Duxford had a grass runway of 800 yards, and, with the poor take off and on landing the poor braking effect of a coarse pitch propeller, we needed every yard of it. I was astounded at the boldness of Squadron Leader Cozens in conducting formation landings at night in this aircraft, especially as the lighting consisted of Great War style paraffin flares.

In spite of the war, most of September 1939 was given over to practice flying, formation, high altitude and night flying. The blacking out of all towns and villages made this harder than we expected. In February 1940 one of our most experienced pilots, Pilot Officer Trenchard, was killed in a night flying accident.

By October we were operational, going forward to spend the days at the bomber airfield at Watton in tents and forbidden the Officers' Mess because the CO did not like the way we fighter pilots looked in our flying boots and heavy sweaters – ready for unheated and unpressurised flight at high altitude. It was still very much a peacetime air force in many ways.

On October 20th we made a sudden move to Catterick, with groundcrews and equipment being carried in four engine Ensign transports. This was in response to the German attack on the Firth of Forth, each squadron moving north one stage. We did a few convoy protection patrols near Flamborough Head and returned to Duxford a week later.

In November we started to patrol from the new Norwich airfield at Horsham St Faith. The mess was not ready and we all lived in a house called 'Redroofs'. There was no night flying so our social life was active. When we were at Horsham on a Sunday we gave an unofficial flying display at low level for the local population. This system of forward basing and coastal patrols continued throughout December and into January 1940.

The flying conditions over this period were often very frightening, there being no proper homing or landing aids and a very poor and outdated cockpit radio. After a spell above cloud you let down gently and hoped that you were over the sea or fens. Sometimes the ground did not show up until you got to 300 feet, when the problem became one of trying to recognise somewhere in rain and mist. A lovelorn Section Leader, Flying Officer Matheson, nearly did for me in these conditions when he took us back from Horsham in terrible weather so as to keep a date in Cambridge!

By March the weather was better but we now had Flying Officer Douglas Bader to contend with. He was very brave and determined but having a hard time coming to terms with the Spitfire, especially in cloud. More than once my friend Watson and I, lent to him as a formation by the CO, emerged from cloud faithfully following Bader, only to find ourselves in a steep diving turn!

This was, of course, the 'Phoney War' period when the war must have often seemed surreal. On May 10th, 1940, all that changed, however, when Hitler attacked the West.

The following day, 19 Squadron scored its first kill, a Ju 88 destroyed over the sea by Flight Lieutenant Wilf Clouston, Flying Officer Petre and Flight Sergeant Harry Steere. Flight Lieutenant Gordon Sinclair:

Brian Lane was a very quiet person, rather intellectual, and always in the background was the fact of his blind father. In his quite way he was a compelling leader, particularly since he was an excellent pilot. We became friends very soon after he came to Duxford, so close that he married Eileen Ellison. quietly and without fuss, to whom I had introduced him! I remember he had a delightful sense of humour and was quick to laugh, he smiled easily. I have thought about Brian frequently since those days.

On 18 May 1940, the Rev'd Fred Jeeves married Brian and Eileen at Great Shelford, the bride's home village. The witnesses were the bride's parents, Sidney, a solicitor, and Theresa. The groom was twenty-three, the bride twenty-eight and a beautiful, quite incredible, woman.

Eileen's family was a wealthy one, this good fortune facilitating her brother's interest in motor sport. The thrills and spills captivated Eileen who began racing herself with an amateur driver, T.P. Cholmondley Tapper, while Tony Ellison acted as their mechanic. The threesome travelled to race meets all over Europe, but Eileen's greatest win was at Brooklands, in 1932, when she won the Duchess of York's race for women drivers. In clinching this victory she beat Kay Petre, the most famous female racing driver of the day.

The military situation on the continent was rapidly deteriorating however, and on 26 May the decision was made to retire on Dunkirk and evacuate Lord Gort's Expeditionary Force. With great foresight and reflecting his determination to keep base secure, Air Chief Marshal Dowding had only committed Hurricanes, which were more plentiful but inferior to the Spitfire in performance, to action on the continent. Having preserved his precious Spitfires for home defence, the time had now come for them to be pitched into battle during Operation DYNAMO, the air operation in support of the evacuation. On 25 May, and in anticipation of the evacuation, Fighter Command moved certain Spitfire squadrons to 11 Group airfields within range of the French and Belgian coast. 19 Squadron was sent to Hornchurch, and on the following day Squadron Leader Stephenson led his Spitfires into action over Calais. There a gaggle of Stukas were found, so the Spitfires throttled right back, matching their targets' speed, as the CO ordered attacks in sections of three. Michael Lyne:

As a former CFS A1 instructor, Stephenson was a precise flier and obedient to the book, which stipulated an overtaking speed of 30 m.p.h. What the book did not foresee, however, was that we would attack Ju 87s doing just 130 m.p.h. The CO led his Section, Pilot Officer Watson No 2 and myself No 3, straight up behind the Ju 87s which looked very relaxed and probably thought we were their fighter escort. The leader of the German fighters, however, had been very clever and pulled his formation away towards England, so that when the dive-bombers turned in towards Calais, the 109s would be protecting their rear. Meanwhile Stephenson realised that we were closing far too fast. I remember his call 'No 19 Squadron! Prepare to attack!', then, to Watson and I in Red Section, 'Throttling back, throttling back.' We were virtually formating on the last section of Ju 87s, and an incredibly slow and dangerous speed in the presence of enemy fighters, and behind us staggered the rest of 19 Squadron at a similar speed. Still the Stukas had not recognised us as a threat, so Stephenson told us to take a target each and fire. So far as I know we must have got the last three, we could hardly have done otherwise, then I broke away as the last section of 109s came round. After the break I was alone and looking for friends when I came under fire for the first time. The first signs were mysterious corkscrews of smoke passing my starboard wing. Then I heard a slow thump, thump, and realised that I was being attacked by a 109 firing machine-guns with tracer and cannons banging away. I broke away sharpish and lost him.

I made a wide sweep and came back to the Calais area to find about five Ju 87s going round in a tight defensive circle. As the 109s had disappeared I had to take the circle head on, giving it a long squirt. At this stage I was hit by return fire, for when I got hack to Hornchurch I found bullet holes in the wing, which had punctured a tyre. Alas my friend Watson was never seen again. Stephenson made a forced landing in France and was captured.

Pilot Officer Peter Howard-Williams was a new pilot on 19 Squadron who had been tasked with collecting and delivering replacement aircraft, as he was not yet 'combat ready':

On May 26th I remember the CO and Watson going missing, Michael Lyne being shot up and Flying Officer Eric Ball landing back at Hornchurch where he found that an enemy bullet had gone through his helmet, parting his hair and leaving a small wound!

For 19 Squadron, the fighting that day was far from over. With the CO missing. It fell to the senior flight commander, Flight Lieutenant Brian Lane, to lead the Squadron into action. Brian later wrote in his log book of ensuing events:

Leading Squadron on patrol of Dunkirk and Calais. Green Section reported eight Me 109s just above us, off Calais. Observed Me 109 chasing Sinclair into cloud. Hun pulled up and gave me a sitting target from below. Gave him a good burst which he ran straight into, lurched and went straight down. I followed him but he hadn't pulled out at 3,000 feet and must have gone straight in. Blacked out completely but pulled out in time. Landed at Manston and stayed for tea. Lovely near the coast in this weather.

Flying Officers Sinclair and Petre also claimed 109s destroyed, but Sergeant Irwin was missing and Pilot Officer Michael Lyne had been shot up again, this time crash landing on Walmer Beach in Kent with a bullet in his knee.

The pathos of action remained constant over the next few days, with Flight Lieutenant Lane still leading 19 Squadron in the air. In the morning of 27 May, 19 Squadron again patrolled high over Dunkirk and Calais, Brian Lane's Section attacking a He 111 over Gravelines. Heavy AA fire, probably 'friendly', nearly, in Brian's words, 'wrote the Squadron off'. All of 19 Squadron's Spitfire returned with flak damage, but were up in the afternoon on a sweep inland to Ypres. Near Dunkirk the Spitfires happened across a lone Hs 126 reconnaissance aircraft which was brought down by Flight Sergeant Unwin. Brian added in his log book: 'I have never seen anything so peaceful – no sign of war at all except the big smoke pall over Dunkirk.'

On 28 May, 19 Squadron began operating as part of a wing formation with 54 and 65 Squadrons. This was because Air Vice-Marshal Keith Park, the Air Officer Commanding 11 Group, unlike his peers, actually knew how to fly a modern fighter aircraft and had observed the fighting over Dunkirk from the cockpit of his personal Hurricane, O-K1. As a result of this, Park recognized that stronger offensive patrols would reduce both losses to his fighters and the effect of enemy attacks on the soldiers below.

The following day saw Squadron Leader 'Tubby' Mermagen's 222 Squadron and Squadron Leader Robin Hood's 41 Squadron arrive at Hornchurch. As 19 Squadron was the most experienced, Brian Lane and his boys led the five-squadron-strong wing, which also included 54 and 65 Squadrons, over the Channel. It must be appreciated, however, that a 'wing' in this sense was only, in effect, a convoy of fighter aircraft travelling together and arriving in the combat area en masse. Moreover, after battle was joined there was no tactical cohesion whatsoever due to the fact that radio communication between squadrons was impossible because each used a different frequency. The squadrons were also operating beyond range of radio contact with their base and therefore did not enjoy the benefit of early radar generated information. This was significant, as in the absence of radar assistance Park's fighters had to mount exhausting standing patrols from dawn to dusk. Due to the logistics and numbers of available Spitfires, there were also problems in maintaining squadron strengths: four squadron wings regularly numbered thirty and not the intended forty-four aircraft. Nevertheless, Air Vice-Marshal Park was responding to a situation for which there was no precedent, and did so rapidly and effectively, his experience over Dunkirk reinforcing his belief that it was better to spoil the aim of many, rather than destroy a few.

On 1 June, Flight Lieutenant Lane led 19, 41, 222 and 616 Squadrons across the Channel; on the first of two sorties that day the wing encountered twelve Me 110s, in Brian's words 'straight from Flying Training School, I should think. Terrific sport!' He destroyed one of the enemy machines, which was last seen streaming coolant at fifty feet, and saw other 110s crash into the sea and on the foreshore. Of the scene below, Brian's log book remarks:

Dunkirk beaches. Most amazing sight, this evacuation. Thames barges, sailing boats, anything that will float, and the Navy. God help them down there! They need more than we can give them.

By 3 June 1940, the evacuation was complete, some 224,686 British and 141,445 French and Belgian troops having been snatched to safety. The following day 19 Squadron left Hornchurch, Flight Lieutenant Lane in Spitfire N3040, which he had flown on all but two sorties over Dunkirk. Later he wrote in his log book: 'Squadron returned to Duxford. Visibility so good that I couldn't see Duxford anywhere! Did a 19 peel off and then peeled off on 48 hours leave. Pretty good.'

During Operation DYNAMO, 19 Squadron had learned much, not least that the tried but untested 'book' was useless. After Squadron Leader Stephenson was captured in the Squadron's first full formation combat over Calais on 26 May, Flight Lieutenant Lane had to suddenly step into the breach, assuming an unexpected responsibility beyond both his years and experience. He responded to this challenge perfectly, leading 19 Squadron on virtually every patrol, and opening his personal account against the enemy. Indeed, the twenty-two-year-old had not just flown at the head of 19 Squadron, but equally so in front of several senior squadron commanders as he led the wing across to France. This swift introduction to combat flying and leadership had been a challenge, which Brian Lane had overcome without mishap or complaint. It would stand him in good stead for the events of a few weeks later.

On 3 June, while 19 Squadron was still at Hornchurch, command of 19 Squadron was officially given to Squadron Leader Phillip

Campbell Pinkham, who joined his new Squadron at Duxford. Pinkham was a regular air force career officer commissioned in 1935. After his service flying training, he flew Gauntlet biplane fighters with 17 Squadron at Kenley, but just six months later joined the Meteorological Flight based at Mildenhall, recording weather data. In January 1938, 'Tommy' Pinkham became a fighter instructor at Andover. There he flew a modern monoplane fighter, a Hurricane, for the first time on 21 March 1939. A year later he was awarded an Air Force Cross in the King's Birthday Honours List for his work training Fins and Poles. Like many other substantive squadron leaders serving in training units, Pinkham had requested a combat command upon the outbreak of war, a good career move providing that one survived. When Squadron Leader Stephenson was captured on 26 May, Squadron Leader Pinkham's name happened to be in the right place on the list.

It is interesting at this point to compare the experience of Squadron Leader Pinkham and Flight Lieutenant Lane. Both were pre-war regular officers, Pinkam three years older than Lane and already a substantive squadron leader. Although he had been a peacetime fighter pilot, flying biplanes, Pinkham, however, had flown for the majority of his service in a non-operational training role. Lane's entire service had been spent as a fighter pilot, firstly on biplanes, then on Hurricanes and Spitfires. He was operationally and tactically aware, popular on the Squadron, and a good pilot. Brian had been a Flight Lieutenant and commander of 19 Squadron's 'A' Flight for nine months. His leadership of the Squadron over Dunkirk, in spite of difficult circumstances, had been absolutely outstanding, so many believed that Brian Lane would be the automatic choice to take over 19 Squadron after Geoffrey Stephenson was captured. The Air Ministry, however, had yet to realize that such quick promotions were essential in wartime so as to have the best and most experienced officer in command, not just the most senior.

On 22 June, 1940, the Battle of France ended when French delegates signed the Armistice with Nazi Germany in a railway carriage at Compiegne. Back at Duxford, 19 Squadron was pressed into a night-fighting in an attempt to counter the threat represented by nocturnal raiders. On the night of 18 June, Flying Officers Johnnie Petre and Eric Ball each destroyed a He 111. Petre, however, had been hit by return fire, as a result of which his Spitfire literally blew up in his face. Although he baled out safely, the young pilot received terribly disfiguring burns.

The German bomber shot down by Flying Officer Petre was flown by Oberleutnant von Arnim, whose father was later a prominent German general in North Africa. Flying Officer Frank Brinsden:

The crew of the He 111 destroyed by Johnnie Petre were held captive in the Officers' Mess. Eileen Lane happened to appear, looking for Brian, and unwittingly shown into the Ladies Room by the Duty Officer – unwittingly because within was being held one of the Germans who, upon Eileen's entry, rose to his feet and greeted her; before the war they had been friends on the continental motor racing circuit!

On 1 July, Squadron Leader Pinkham examined Flight Lieutenant Lane's flying log book. Therein he saw that since 1 June 1939, this bright young officer had flown a total of 189.30 hours, 14.05 hours of which were at night, giving a grand total of 732.35 hours. 19 Squadron's new CO endorsed the log as being that of an 'Exceptional fighter pilot' who was 'above the average' as an aerial marksman. Very few pilots receive an 'exceptional' rating; clearly Squadron Leader Pinkham recognized the ability, experience and potential of his senior flight commander.

On 22 July, a new policy commenced of sending Brian Lane's 'A' Flight from Fowlmere, in the Duxford Sector, to Coltishall on a daily detachment. The purpose was to assist 66 Squadron in providing convoy protection patrols. The 19 Squadron pilots were pleased with this development as they hoped that operating near the coast would give them a greater chance on contacting the enemy. The unit, as the RAF's most experienced Spitfire squadron, was often used to test new equipment, and had recently been re-equipped with the Spitfire Mk IB. This variant was identical to the Mk IA except that all eight Browning machine-guns had been removed and replaced with two 20 mm Hispano Suiza cannons. The Me 109, of course, was already armed with two 7.9 mm Rheinmetal-Borsig machine-guns and two 20 mm Oerlikon cannons, this mixed weaponry providing the enemy pilot with the benefits of both rapid firing machine-guns and hard hitting cannon. Behind in the arms race, Fighter Command was now desperate to give its pilots similar firepower, hence the Mk IB being rushed into service with 19 Squadron; a smaller number also went to 92 Squadron at Biggin Hill.

Squadron Leader Pinkham has often been criticized for having busied himself with evaluating the new Spitfire, while Flight Lieutenant Lane continued to lead 19 Squadron in the air. This, however, is actually further evidence of Brian Lane's ability and the confidence that could be placed in him. The cannon-armed Spitfires were problematic, and yet the Spitfire pilots were in desperate need of this hard hitting weapon. Resolution of stoppages was therefore a priority, and it was right that the CO, who was after all a very experienced pilot, should take on the job himself. This he was able to do only because of having such an able deputy in Brian Lane, who could be relied upon completely to lead the Squadron operationally while the CO was otherwise engaged.

News received on 31 July gave 19 Squadron cause for celebration: Brian Lane had been awarded the Distinguished Flying Cross. Pilot Officer Wallace 'Jock' Cunningham remembers:

> Shortly after Brian's DFC came through for his good leadership of the Squadron and general activities at Dunkirk, we were lying in the sun at Coltishall along with Squadron Leader Douglas Bader and other 242 Squadron pilots. Douglas was kidding Brian and asked him 'What's that?', in his usual cocky fashion, pointing to Brian's DFC ribbon. 'I must get one of those!', said Bader, and, as we all know, he later did.

Although command of 19 Squadron had been given to another officer, it was fitting indeed that Flight Lieutenant Lane's efforts should at least be recognized with the award of a gallantry decoration.

The largely uneventful and boring convoy protection patrols continued into August, the 12 Group pilots becoming increasingly frustrated at their lack of action when compared to the casualties being taken by their counterparts in 11 Group. The Spitfire Mk IBs were also proving unpopular because the cannons jammed so regularly. Without any other armament this left the pilot unable to defend himself, so confidence in the cannon-armed Spitfires was low. The cannon, which weighed 96 pounds, was designed to be mounted upright, but due to the Spitfire's thin wing section it was necessary to fit the weapon on its side, meaning the spent shell cases were ejected from that direction, instead of from below as the manufacturer intended. 19 Squadron's armourers carried out sterling work by designing and fitting deflector plates, but still the problem was not entirely solved, the empty shell not being thrown clear of the cannon but bouncing back into it; the next incoming round then jammed the offending case in the breech, rendering the weapon inoperable.

On 11 August, Spitfire X4231 was delivered to the Squadron, this being the first aircraft fitted with the 'B' wing, combining a cannon with two Browning machine-guns. It was feared that the machine-guns' extra weight would make the aircraft under powered, but a test flight by Squadron Leader Pinkham proved this to be a groundless concern. Although all agreed that the new armament combination was a step in the right direction, tellingly the 19 Squadron diary comments that: 'Possibly another step in the same direction would be re-equipping with the old eight-gun machines.'

By this time the Battle of Britain raged over southern England; on 16 August, 'A' Flight of 19 Squadron encountered the enemy en masse for the first time since Dunkirk. Brian Lane's log book records:

> Returning from Coltishall investigated X Raid above cloud with
> seven aircraft of 'A' Flight. Turned out to be about *150* Huns!!
> Waded into escort of Me 110s but ruddy cannons stopped on me.

Upon being attacked the 110s went into a defensive circle. Although
the Spitfire pilots destroyed three 110s, six of the seven Spitfires
suffered cannon stoppages. Pilot Officer Cunningham, who shot
down a 110: 'I recall mainly Sergeant "Jimmy" Jennings on the
R/T bemoaning his jammed 20 mm cannon, full of indignation
at the unfairness of life in general.' The Squadron diary reflected
that: 'Results would have been doubled had we been equipped
with either cannon and machine-guns or just eight machine-
guns.' Fortunately for 'A' Flight, although escorting Me 109s were
present, for some reason they did not attack.

On Saturday 24 August, six large raids were mounted against
England, the fourth of which reached the East End at 3 p.m. 11
Group called for assistance from 12 Group, and 19 Squadron, led
by Flight Lieutenant Lane, was scrambled to intercept an incoming
formation of fifty enemy aircraft. Brian recorded events in his log
book:

> Ran into a bunch of Huns over estuary. Had a bang at an Me
> 110 but had to break away as tracer was coming over my head
> from another behind me. He appeared to be hitting his fellow
> countryman in front of me but I didn't wait to see if he shot him
> down. Had a crack at another and shot his engine right out of the
> wing – lovely! Crashed near North Foreland. Last trip in 'Blitzen
> III'.

When the cannons worked, there was no doubting their effectiveness. Only two of the nine 19 Squadron pilots engaged had been able to expend all of their ammunition without a stoppage, which was clearly unacceptable.

During this phase of the Battle of Britain, the Luftwaffe was pounding 11 Group airfields, hitting Sector Stations like Biggin Hill, Hornchurch and Kenley very hard. On 26 August, 11 Group again called for assistance; Sergeant David Cox:

Again Brian Lane led us off. We were ordered to patrol at 10,000 feet, but the Observer Corps reported the raid incoming at 1,000 feet. The 11 Group controllers thought this to be a mistake, so we were told to remain at 10,000 feet. The raid came and went and but we were blissfully unaware and therefore did not engage. The subsequent intelligence report stated that the 'Spitfires from Fowlmere were slow in getting off the ground', which was certainly not the case.

On 31 August, Brian Lane and the rest of 'A' Flight were enjoying a rare day off duty. 'B' Flight, however, intercepted a raid on Duxford. Although victories were claimed, it was a costly combat for Flight Lieutenant Wilf Clouston's pilots: Flying Officer James Coward was shot down in X4231, baling out missing a foot, and Flying Officer Frank Brinsden also went over the side, being violently ill during his subsequent parachute descent and so drenched in petrol that he was lucky not to catch fire. nineteen-year-old Pilot Officer Aeberhardt crash landed at Fowlmere with a damaged aircraft but was killed. Again the Squadron diary was critical of the cannons: 'The score would most definitely been higher given eight machine-guns.' By now the pilots had completely lost confidence in the Mk IB, so much so that Flight Lieutenant Lane made representation, on behalf of all pilots, to Squadron Leader Pinkham who consequently requested that 19 Squadron be re-equipped with Mk IAs. Duxford's Station Commander and 'Boss' Controller, Group Captain A.B. 'Woody' Woodhall, supported this view and endorsed Pinkham's report to Fighter Command HQ:

> I got on the phone to Leigh-Mallory and urgently requested that 19 Squadron should have its eight-gun Spitfires back. The following afternoon the Commander-in-Chief himself landed at Duxford, without warning. I greeted him and he gruffly said 'I want to talk to 19 Squadron', so I drove him over to Fowlmere. There he met Sandy Lane and other pilots. He listened to their complaints almost in silence, then I drove him back to his aircraft which he was piloting personally. As he climbed into the aeroplane he merely said 'You'll get your eight-gun Spitfires back.' 'Stuffy' Dowding was a man of few words; he listened to all of us, asked a few pertinent questions, then made his decision: As a result, that same evening the instructors from the operational training unit at Hawarden flew their eight-gun Spitfires down and exchanged them for IBs.

While 'A' Flight was re-equipping, on 3 September Squadron Leader Pinkham led 'B' Flight on a standing patrol over Duxford and Debden. The Spitfires were vectored to North Weald, but arrived to find that the Sector Station had already been bombed. Flying in pairs line astern, 19 Squadron attacked the withdrawing enemy from above and ahead. The combat was Pinkham's first, in which he suffered cannon stoppage and made no claim, but Me

110s were destroyed by Flying Officer Haines and Flight Sergeant Unwin. For the rest of that day, 611 Squadron, sent down from Ternhill to Fowlmere, covered 19 Squadron's patrols while the exchange of Spitfires was completed.

On 4 September, Squadron Leader Pinkham led 19 Squadron firstly on a patrol over Debden, then on another over Debden, North Weald and Hornchurch Sector Stations. The sorties were uneventful but the Squadron diarist, while bemoaning the tired aircraft from Hawarden, appeared more optimistic for the future: 'First day with eight-gun machines, and what wrecks. At least the guns will fire!'

The following morning, Squadron Leader Pinkham and 19 Squadron were up over Hornchurch. Over the patrol area, Sergeant Jennings sighted a formation of forty Do 17s escorted by forty Me 109s, all incoming over the Thames Estuary. The CO was at first unable to see the enemy, so Jennings directed events until Pinkham had the bandits in sight and ordered Brian Lane's 'A' Flight to attack the 109s while he personally led 'B' Flight against the bombers. 'B' Flight engaged the Do 17s in pairs, from the rear, but at that moment high flying 109s fell on Pinkham and his tiny force. A classic cut-and-thrust fighter-to-fighter combat developed, as the whole of 19 Squadron became embroiled with the 109s. Flying Officer Haines pursued a 1/JG 54 109 across Kent, on the deck, the German fighter eventually crashing onto 6 Hardy Street, Maidstone, and the Czech Sergeant Plzak left another 109 pouring black smoke. Two Spitfires were damaged, however, and Squadron Leader Pinkham failed to return. Later a Spitfire that had crashed in the remote countryside near Birling in Kent was identified as Pinkham's, his body being found nearby. It was believed that the

19 Squadron CO had been hit by a cross-fire from a vic of Do 17s, and possibly also hit by a 109. Apparently the twenty-five-year-old Spitfire pilot had tried to bale out, but due to wounds to his chin, chest and hip had great difficulty in doing so; by the time he abandoned the doomed aircraft it was too low for his parachute to open. Brian Lane wrote:

A gloom descended over the Mess and there wasn't quite so much talking or laughter as usual, as we sat drinking after supper that night. Next day, after lunch, Russell, our Adjutant, rang me up.

'Keep this under your hat until Woody rings up, but you've got the Squadron. Congratulations!'

'Shut up and stop blathering,' I said.

'No, really. After all, you've had the Squadron once before so I suppose they think you might as well try to make a mess of it again!'

'I don't want any of your rudeness, Budd,' I said coldly, using his surname. He laughed.

'Good Lord, I shall have to salute you now, I suppose!'

And so it was that Brian Lane added his 'scraper' ring to his uniform sleeves, indicating that he was, at last, a squadron leader, although, typically, Brian also wrote that this was a 'sad promotion' given the circumstances. Wing Commander George Unwin:

Brian Lane was a first class pilot and leader. He was firstly my Flight Commander, and then my Squadron CO. He was completely unflappable and instilled confidence in all who flew with him.

Having led 19 Squadron on the vast majority of operational flights since 26 May, there could have been no better choice for Squadron Leader Pinkham's successor than Brian Lane.

The role of 12 Group, in which the Duxford Sector Station was situated, during the Battle of Britain was to defend the industrial Midlands and the North, in addition to providing assistance to 11 Group as and when required. The System dictated that on occasions when 11 Group's squadrons were engaged, 12 Group would cover 11 Group's airfields. Such a protective umbrella was clearly essential, but certain 12 Group pilots found it unacceptable that they should be employed in such a mundane way while Group pilots were so heavily engaged. On 30 August, Squadron Leader Douglas Bader's 242 Squadron was scrambled from Duxford to intercept a raid on Hatfield, in 11 Group. The Hurricanes acquitted themselves well, scoring several victories, convincing Bader that had he more fighters in the air then the score would have been greater. This theory received support from Group Captain Woodhall and Air Vice-Marshal Leigh-Mallory, Air Officer Commander-in-Chief of 12 Group. Consequently it was arranged that Bader would lead the '12 Group Wing', based at Duxford and comprising the Spitfires of 19 Squadron, and the Hurricanes of both 242 and 310. The concept was not to merely defend 11 Group's airfields but to offensively seek out and engage the enemy in strength. This was contrary to the System, and the opposite of 11 Group's tactic involving small numbers of fighters harrying the enemy both incoming and outgoing, which was working. In this way 11 Group's fighters were never presented in numbers to the enemy, to be destroyed by the numerically greater Me 109s. The completely contrary 'Big Wing' concept, however, was, recent research proves, based upon a misconception from the outset: on 30 August 1940, the Hatfield raiders were not attacked purely by 242 Squadron, as Squadron Leader Bader had assumed, but also by Hurricanes and Spitfires of 11 Group. The more fighters are in the air then the greater becomes the over claiming factor, as pilots independently attack the same aircraft oblivious of each other; consequently that enemy machine ends up being credited to various pilots and therefore the overall score becomes greatly inflated. Therefore 242 Squadron did not actually inflict the level of damage that it believed, and actual enemy losses were, in fact, shared between many RAF fighters. Douglas Bader, though, as ever believed that he was 100 per cent correct, and his enthusiasm and strong personality won over his seniors.

On Saturday 7 September, the Germans made a huge tactical blunder: having pounded 11 Group's airfields for several weeks, at what was the crucial point the Luftwaffe changed its target and bombed London. When a huge raid came in that afternoon, Air Chief Marshal Dowding assumed that airfields were again the target and knew that such a gigantic attack could well deliver a telling blow. The German formation did not separate into smaller groups, each attacking a different target, but continued along the Thames Estuary. Eventually it became clear to Fighter Command's confused Controllers that the target was London. The Duxford Wing was already up, patrolling over North Weald, and urgently vectored south. Some fifteen miles north of the Thames anti-aircraft fire could be seen bursting around twenty bombers, escorted by fighters, heading west at 15,000 feet. The 12 Group fighters were lower than the enemy and as Bader climbed his force to attack, the enemy fighters pounced. Squadron Leader Brian Lane:

An Me 110 dived in front of me and I led 'A' Flight after it. Two Hurricanes were also attacking it. I fired a short burst at it, the other aircraft attacking at the same time. The crew of two baled out, one parachute failing to open. The E/A crashed one mile east of Hornchurch and one of the crew landed nearby and was seen to be taken prisoner.

As is so often the case in aerial combat, after this engagement Squadron Leader Lane, Flight Lieutenant Lawson and Sergeant Jennings found themselves all alone. Unable to re-locate the scene of action, the three Spitfires returned to Fowlmere. Caught on the climb, 242 and 310 Squadrons had not fared well: Bader himself had been shot up, Sub-Lieutenant Dickie Cork was slightly wounded and Pilot Officer Benzie was missing; one of 310's pilots was terribly burned and another forced landed near Southend. A disappointed Bader reported that his formation had been requested too late by the 11 Group Controller, as a result of which it had been bounced while climbing; he later wrote: 'It was windy work, let there be no mistake.'

Two days later the Wing was in action again, this time with much better results, claiming the destruction of twenty enemy aircraft offset against the loss of four Hurricanes with two pilots killed. We now know that the figure of twenty enemy aircraft destroyed was grossly inaccurate, the actual number being nearer five. Nevertheless the figure of twenty enemy machines destroyed was accepted without question, leading to various congratulatory signals and more squadrons being absorbed into the Duxford effort.

On 11 September, 242 Squadron remained at Coltishall and did not fly down to operate from Duxford. The 'Big Wing' went up, however, and was led over London by Squadron Leader Lane:

> Party over London. 19 leading 611 & 74 Squadrons. Sighted a big bunch of Huns south of the river and got a lovely head on attack into leading Heinkels. We broke them up and picked on a small bunch of six with two Me 110s as escort. I found myself entirely alone with these lads so proceeded to have a bit of sport. Got one of the Me 110s on fire, whereupon the other left his charges and ran for home! Played with He 111s for a bit and finally got one in both engines. Never had so much fun before!

September 15th is now celebrated annually as 'Battle of Britain Day'. Between 11.33 and 11.35 a.m. that fateful day, three huge German formations crossed the south coast between Dover and Folkestone, London bound. 11 Group had twenty squadrons in the air to meet this threat, reinforcing them at mid-day with the Duxford Wing, now consisting of two Spitfire and three Hurricane squadrons. Bader sallied forth and attacked twenty-four Do 17s of KG 76, escorted by Me 109s, at 16,000 feet over Brixton. One particular Dornier was attacked by numerous 12 Group fighters, including Brian Lane, who saw the enemy crew bale out and their bomber crash in Kent.

In the afternoon the Wing was scrambled again, making a total of thirty-one RAF fighter squadrons in action over London; we can only imagine the adverse effect of such a sight on enemy morale, German aircrews having been assured that the British were down to their 'last fifty Spitfires'. Again the Wing was too low, and again attacked by Me 109s while feverishly climbing. Brian Lane's log book:

Party. 242 leading Wing. Ran into the whole Luftwaffe over London. Wave after wave of bombers covered by several hundred fighters. Waded into escort as per arrangement and picked out a 109. Had one hell of a dogfight and finally he went into cloud inverted and obviously crashed as he appeared out of control.

In what was a confused mass of many fighters, Brian's engagement with the 109 represented the only protracted individual dogfight that day. His combat report describes vents in greater detail:

I was leading 19 Squadron on Wing patrol. At approximately 1440 hours AA fire was sighted to the south and at the same time a formation of about 30 Do 215s was seen. I climbed up astern of the enemy aircraft to engage the fighter escort which could be seen above the bombers at about 30,000 feet. Three Me 109s dived on our formation and I turned to starboard. A loose dogfight ensued with more Me 109s coming down. I could not go near to any enemy aircraft so I climbed up and engaged a formation of Me 110s without result. I then sighted 10 Me 109s just above me and I attacked one of them. I got on his tail and fired several bursts of about two seconds. The enemy aircraft was taking violent evasive action and made for cloud level. I managed to get in another burst of about five seconds before it flicked over inverted and entered cloud in a shallow dive, apparently out of control. I then flew south and attacked two further formations of about 30 Do 215s from astern and head on. The enemy aircraft did not appear to like head on attack as they jumped about a bit as I passed through. I observed no result from these attacks. Fire from rear of the enemy aircraft was opened at 1,000 yards. Me 110s opened fire at a similar range and appeared to have no idea of deflection shooting.

Back at Duxford the 12 Group Wing's total claims were 45 enemy aircraft destroyed, 3 shared, 10 probables and another damaged. In total Fighter Command claimed 175 German aircraft destroyed, offset against the loss of 30 aircraft and 10 pilots. In fact the Luftwaffe had lost only 56 aircraft, of which the Duxford Wing actually accounted for 15. Nonetheless the fighting that day was decisive: by dusk, despite Göring's assurances, Hitler was convinced that the Luftwaffe was unable to win the aerial supremacy required for his proposed invasion.

The Battle of Britain was not yet over, however. Friday 27 September, for example was another day of heavy fighting. Squadron Leader Lane's take-off was delayed due to technical problems, so Flight Lieutenant Lawson led 19 Squadron into action against 'innumerable' enemy fighters over Canterbury. As battle was joined, Brian caught up with the Wing and fired two short bursts at a 109. His Spitfire then became uncontrollable, skidding away. The pilot contemplated taking to his parachute but, using all his strength, managed to regain control and levelled out at 3,000 feet. Back at Fowlmere it was discovered that the offending Spitfire, a new Mk II, had a misshapen rudder and an incorrectly adjusted trim tab which prevented one elevator from, functioning correctly. It was a lucky escape for our hero.

The Battle of Britain is officially considered to have ended on 31 October 1940. By that time the Germans had become increasingly forced to bomb by night, the RAF having maintained control of the daylight sky, although the two fighter forces continued to clash-until early 1941. In November, the Duxford Wing continued flying numerous patrols over London and southern England. On Friday 8 November, German fighter sweeps were again met with fierce opposition. Squadron Leader Lane led 19 Squadron on a Wing patrol over Canterbury, as Wing Commander Bernard 'Jimmy' Jennings, then a Sergeant pilot, remembered:

We were over Canterbury and I was flying as Sandy Lane's No 2. We were told that there was a party going on above us which could not see as the sky was covered by a layer of 8/10 thinnish cloud. Sandy put us into a climb, and as we were nearing the cloud base an Me 109 dived out of the cloud a short distance in front of us, followed by a Hurricane firing his guns even closer, in fact over the top of Sandy and myself. Sandy's engine was hit, packed up and he lost height. As his No 2, and because there were obviously some unfriendly people were about, I stayed with him.

Once we were clear of trouble I called up Sandy and suggested that he held his gliding course and I would go ahead and find somewhere for him to land. I said 'Waggle your wings if you hear me'. He did so and I dived away only to find the airfield at Eastchurch bombed and unusable. However, there was a small strip clear of bomb craters. I flew back up to Sandy and asked him to follow me. He did, and taking one look at the state of the airfield rightly decided to land wheels up.

He crash landed his Spitfire OK, but as I circled over him I could see Sandy in the cockpit, not moving. I looked round the airfield until I saw an air raid shelter which I beat up until two airmen poked their heads out of the entrance. I pointed towards Sandy and then circled him and saw the airmen go behind a shelter to get into a truck. I circled Sandy again and saw him getting out of his aircraft, holding his face with one hand and waving to me with the other. I waited until the truck had picked him up and then returned to base.

I told everybody that Brian was safe and told his wife that I would fetch him the next day in the Magister. We got a message through to Eastchurch to that effect. Early next morning I flew the Magister to Hornchurch and after some argument with Sector Control managed to get permission to collect Sandy from Eastchurch. After circling low over the airfield a truck brought Sandy to the small strip which I had seen the previous day. I landed but as Sandy walked towards me I burst out laughing as he had a very puffed up nose! In order to keep an eye on the Squadron following him, Brian used to fly with his shoulder straps very loose. He forgot to tighten them before his crash landing and hit his face on the gunsight.

In his logbook, of this 'Friendly Fire' incident, Brian Lane wrote:

I sighted Me 109s over Canterbury and turned to give chase. Hurricane squadron chased us and the leader put a burst into my engine!! Apparently the CO of one of the North Weald squadrons. Force landed at Eastchurch OK. Jennings escorted me down and refused to leave me. Damn good of him.

The offending Hurricane pilot was Squadron Leader Lionel Gaunce, CO of North Weald's 46 Squadron. Bader, so the story goes, flew straight over there and remonstrated with Gaunce; ironically, Bader himself became the victim of friendly fire when brought down over France on 9 August 1941.

By this time Air Chief Marshal Dowding had been retired, and Air Vice-Marshal Park sent to Training Command. These two architects of victory had been called to account for their tactics by the Air Ministry on 17 October, Air Vice-Marshal Leigh-Mallory and the 'Big Wing' protagonists having won considerable political support for their flawed theory. Shortly after the meeting Leigh-Mallory took over Park's 11 Group, and Sholto Douglas, the Deputy Chief of the Air Staff, was promoted to succeed Dowding. These two men were now able to push forward wing operations as standard practice, and every Sector Station was organized into a wing. So it was that on 14 November, Squadron Leader Lane led 19 Squadron at the head of the Wittering Wing, comprising Nos. 1 and 266 Squadrons. It was the last of a series of such training flights, but, as Brian's logbook records: 'Nearly last patrol with any wing! Ajax leader led his Squadron straight into us from the sun as we climbed to meet them. Created quite a shambles.'

The following morning saw 19 and 242 Squadrons detailed to patrol a convoy twenty miles east of Harwich. Unfortunately the convoy could not be found, so when Ground Control informed the formation of three bandits approaching from the north-west. Squadron Leader Lane left the Hurricanes to continue searching for the convoy while the faster Spitfires climbed to intercept. Soon two condensation trails were spotted at 35,000 feet, fifteen to twenty miles apart, and the Squadron split into flights to give chase. While 'A' Flight pursued the high-flying intruders, 'B' Flight positioned itself to cut off the enemy's line of retreat. Squadron Leader Lane led Red Section after the leading German and climbed south to get between the enemy aircraft and the sun. The chase up the Thames Estuary lasted twenty minutes, later being described by Brian as a 'Cook's Tour'. Eventually the two Me 110s saw the approaching Spitfires and dived eastward. Red Section attacked in line astern, opening fire from 800 feet. As Brian Lane's bullets found their mark a cowling flew off the 110, which started streaming glycol. Red 2, Pilot Officer Wallace 'Jock' Cunningham, set the starboard engine alight. As the 110 climbed, Brian delivered the fatal blow from the starboard quarter. The enemy machine plunged into the Thames; both crewmen baled out but remain officially missing. Wallace Cunningham:

> I was tucked in behind Brian Lane and diving after the fleeting Me 110. Because of our high speed, Brian was struggling to get his sights on target – I was almost jostling him off to get a chance. Before we eventually destroyed the German aircraft, after letting the crew bale out, I had my windscreen shattered. Not, I worked out later, by the enemy but from Brian's empty cartridge cases.

The winter months continued in much the same vein, with the odd action fought over convoys, the occasional clash with German fighters, and more practice wing formations. The night blitz, however, was reaching its zenith, but Britain's nocturnal defences were woefully inadequate. Even Spitfires, which were poor night flying aircraft given the narrow track undercarriage and two glowing banks of exhausts forward of the pilot which spoiled his night vision, were pressed into service. 'Fighter Nights' were organized in which the sky over London was filled with Spitfires, in the hope that they would sight an enemy bomber. Success was rare, but at least the pilots felt they were doing something to help combat this particular threat, which was taking a great toll of civilian life. Brian Lane and his pilots therefore had this extra duty to undertake in addition to their normal daytime patrols. The crescendo of German night attacks came on the night of 10 May 1941, when 500 enemy bombers dropped 700 tonnes of high explosive and incendiary bombs on London. The raid coincided with a low spring tide, severely limiting the water available to fire fighters. By dawn, over 1,000 Londoners were dead and another 2,000 injured. 19 Squadron were up over London that night but made no contact. Generally night-fighting was improving, however, as aircrews mastered their rudimentary airborne interception radar: in January 1941 only three German bombers were destroyed, in May ninety-six failed to return to their bases in France.

After that terrible raid the activity tailed off as German units were withdrawn and sent eastwards to quickly refit prior to the surprise invasion of Russia on 22 June 1941. Fighter Command was also pursuing an offensive policy, 'Reaching Out' and taking the war to the Germans in northern France, Belgium and Holland. On 21 May, Squadron Leader Lane led 19, 266 and 310 Squadrons to West Malling to participate in a 'Circus' operation. The 12 Group Wing's task was to patrol the south-east coast at 20,000 feet, so as to protect the bombers from attack on their return journey, should the Germans be so bold as to pursue the Blenheims back across the Channel. The operation was completed successfully and 19 Squadron's sortie was uneventful.

On 4 June, Brian led 19 and 266 Squadrons on a sweep of south-east England and the Thames Estuary. Probably due to oxygen failure, Wing Commander William Coope, flying Green Leader with 266 Squadron, crashed into the sea; he remains missing and is remembered on the Runnymede Memorial. The following night, at 1 a.m., Brian took off for a nocturnal patrol only to be recalled ten minutes later in preparation for a 'Fighter Night' over Birmingham. The expected raid failed to materialize, however, so the operation was cancelled. On the night of 14 June, Brian was aloft and saw an enemy aircraft crash in flames, but reported no other contact.

15 June 1941, was a notable day for 19 Squadron: Squadron Leader Brian Lane was being rested, his successor being Squadron Leader Roy Dutton DFC & bar. By that time Brian Lane had flown operations continuously since the outbreak of war, had won a DFC for his leadership of 19 Squadron over Dunkirk, and had flown throughout the Battle of Britain and beyond. It was time for a rest, however reluctantly Brian left his beloved 19 Squadron, and after a short period of leave, reported to No. 12 Group HQ at Watnall for staff duties on 20 June. There he remained, flying a desk, until 11 November, when he embarked on a troop ship, bound for another staff appointment overseas. On 28 January, 1942, he arrived at the Desert Air Force HQ. Unfortunately the unfamiliar climate negatively affected his health, so four months later he was posted back to the UK.

On 16 September 1942, Squadron Leader Lane reported for a refresher course at 61 OTU at Montford Bridge, a satellite of Rednal in Shropshire. There Brian familiarized himself with the

Spitfire Mk V, which enjoyed the benefits of both cannons and machine-guns, and by completion of the course had flown a total of 30.40 hours, 26.50 of which were on Spitfires. Before leaving Montford Bridge, Brian met a 19 Squadron chum by chance in a Cheshire country pub; Frank Brinsden:

> I was up that way learning to fly Mosquitoes and it was a pleasant surprise to meet Brian by chance. He was happy to be back in England flying Spitfires again, and looked forward to the future with optimism. I am sure that with his very great experience it would not have been long before he was appointed as a Wing Leader. Remember that he had actually led wing-sized formations over Dunkirk, long before Douglas Bader came up with his cock-eyed Big Wing theory. Brian would have made an excellent Wing Leader, no doubt about that.

On 9 December 1942, Brian reported to 167 'Gold Coast' Squadron as a supernumerary squadron leader to update his experience of combat conditions prior to his next appointment, which, as Frank says, is likely to have been as a Wing Leader.

167 Squadron was a Dutch unit, with an English CO and other key personnel, based at Ludham, between Norwich and the Norfolk coast. On 26 October, permission was given for Dutch pilots to fly rhubarbs, low level opportunist strafing attacks by a pair or section of Spitfires, but due to poor winter weather no operational sorties had been possible by the time Squadron Leader Lane arrived. His first flight with the inexperienced Squadron was in a Spitfire Mk VB, 3W-H, a local familiarization flight of just thirty minutes duration on the morning of Sunday 13 December.

Later that day, Squadron Leader Lane led a section of 167 Squadron Spitfires on their first Rhubarb to strafe the main Rotterdam to Antwerp railway line between Moerdyk and Bergen-Op-Zoom. The Spitfires left Ludham at 3.10 p.m., bound for their target area situated just beyond a complex system of large inlands and estuaries. As the Spitfires bobbed across the North Sea, light was already fading. At 3.50 p.m. Brian led the Section over the Dutch coast between Voorne and Goeree. Following the Raring Vliet water inland to the Hollandseh Deep estuary at zero feet, as the Spitfires flashed by Helleveotsluis, surprised German flak gunners managed to loose off intense tracer rounds at their fleeting enemy, as did gunners at Willemstad, Moerdyk Bridge and on the northern shore of the Hollandseh Deep. At Moerdyk Brian turned the Section south, flying inland some ten miles, following the railway line to Roosendaal where Blue 4, Pilot Huekensfeldt-Jansen became separated in the fading light. Alone over hostile territory, the Dutch pilot had no option but to observe Standing Orders and return alone to Ludham, his guns unfired. Continuing along the railway line, the three remaining Spitfires found no targets, so Squadron Leader Lane turned the Section about, heading back to base and leaving the Dutch coast over the Ooster Scheldt, still at zero feet.

Suddenly, two miles south of Zierikee on the island of Schouwen, two FW 190s appeared, pursuing the Spitfires and also at zero feet. Blue 3 sighted the bandits but was unable to communicate the threat to Blue 1, Squadron Leader Lane, as his radio was u/s. As the 190s bore down on the Spitfires, Plesman opened up his throttle and flew alongside Brian Lane, warning him of the danger. By now precious seconds had been lost and the superior 190s were within effective firing range. From 300 yards the Germans opened fire on Blue 1 and Blue 2, Pilot Officer W.G. Evans. The Spitfires immediately took violent evasive action, Lane breaking right and Evans breaking left. Meanwhile Plesman had climbed to 2,000 feet and dived upon the leading 190, firing a two second burst in a fleeting head on attack, narrowly avoiding a collision. Before reaching cloud cover Evans managed two bursts at a 190 from long range but without result. Squadron Leader Lane had disappeared, so Plesman broke off his attack to search for Blue 1, spotting the Squadron Leader chasing an enemy fighter inland. This was, of course, the first time that Brian had met the awesome FW 190, but even so he had lost no time in turning the tables and getting on an enemy's tail, chasing it in an easterly direction. As Blue 1 appeared in control of the situation, Plesman hurried to assist Evans, who managed to shake off his assailant, so, the sky now typically empty of aircraft, the two Spitfires returned to Ludham. Having landed at 5 p.m., Plesman and Evans would wait in vain at Ludham for Blue 1's return. Squadron Leader Lane DFC and Spitfire AR612 were missing, Fighter Command's only loss that grey December day.

What happened to this brave and gallant young Spitfire pilot? Many years later I found the answer in German records: Oberleutnant Walter Leonhardt of 6/JG 1 claimed a Spitfire destroyed over the North Sea at 4.34 p.m., twenty miles west of Schouwen Island. This was undoubtedly AR612, and it is not difficult to imagine what had happened: the FW 190 was faster than the Spitfire Mk V, and Brian Lane would have been nearing the end of fuel available for such a chase; eventually he must have had to break off and head for home, and at which point in time the tables were turned. Enjoying superior performance, Leonhardt was able to pursue, catch and destroy AR612, sending aircraft and pilot to a watery grave in the cold North Sea.

The loss of a pilot and leader with Brian Lane's experience on such a futile sortie was a tragedy. Even if the section had found and shot up a train or two, would that have compared to losing a pilot of his quality in the process? I think not, and sadly many pilots were lost on similarly pointless operations. Someone who felt very strongly about this at the time was Johnnie Johnson, later the RAF's top scoring fighter pilot in WW2, who resolved to do something to stop these senseless losses while being rested as a staff officer between tours in 1943. As a result of representation made by Johnnie to the Air Officer Commanding, Rhubarbs were stopped that year, albeit too late to save Squadron Leader Lane and many others like him. Former 19 Squadron pilots remember Brian Lane: Wing Commander George Unwin:

I flew with Brian Lane for a year and we were in complete accord in the air. He was an officer and I was an NCO, so we did not, therefore, associate off duty. However, despite our difference in rank we were good friends. My very last flight with 19 Squadron, prior to taking up instructor duties in Training Command, was formation aerobatics with Brian leading and my very great friend Harry Steere making up the third. Brian Lane was a first class pilot and leader. He was firstly my flight commander, and then the Squadron CO, was completely unflappable and instilled confidence in all who flew with him. It was a sad loss when he was killed.

Wing Commander Bernard Jennings:

Brian Lane was a highly respected squadron commander, a pilot's pilot and an efficient leader respected even by us regular NCO pilots.

Wing Commander David Cox:

Brian Lane was, in my opinion, one of the finest squadron commanders I served under, not only as a fighter leader but also as a man. He was always kind and considerate, and had time for everyone, however lowly their rank. I can illustrate his kindness and consideration by relating something he did for me.

I joined 19 Squadron on May 13th, 1940, but owing to my lack of experience flying Spitfires I was not allowed to operate with the Squadron over Dunkirk. My job was to ferry spare aircraft to Hornchurch or test them after service. On May 28th, after testing a Spitfire for radio trouble, I was preparing to land but found that the undercarriage would not go fully down, sticking half way. After trying unsuccessfully for some time to rectify the situation, which included inverting the aircraft to try and take the weight off the pins, I had to land with the undercart stuck halfway down. The Engineering Officer later put the aircraft in the hangar, jacked it up and the undercarriage worked perfectly. Squadron Leader Pinkham endorsed my log book as follows:

'On August 10th, 1940, Sergeant Cox was charged at Duxford with damaging one of his Majesty's aircraft, namely a Spitfire, through landing with the undercarriage incompletely lowered. CO Duxford directed that he be admonished and ordered me to make this entry.'

I deeply resented this and in a way the incident soured my attitude towards the RAF. During February 1941, when things were quiet, I went to Brian Lane, who by then was our CO, and told him how unjust I felt the endorsement to be as I had done my best to get the undercarriage down. He agreed to look into the matter. I later heard from the Squadron Adjutant that Squadron Leader Lane had taken the matter up at Group HQ and even made a formal visit. The result came several months later when 'Cancelled' was written in red ink across the endorsement. Brian also added below it: 'Entry made in error. No disciplinary action was taken, as accident not attributable to pilot.'

Brian had discovered that there had been similar accidents, caused by an air lock which had been removed by the shock of landing, hence why the undercarriage worked perfectly in the hangar.

If Brian Lane had not been lost in such a useless action, I am sure that he would have been one of the greatest fighter leaders of the war, quite possibly equal to Douglas Bader and Johnnie Johnson. Certainly he was amongst the first pilots with experience of leading wing formation, as evidenced by his activities over Dunkirk. Someone in Fighter Command surely made a blunder in posting him to No 167 Squadron which specialised in low level ground attacks, during which flak was intense and luck played a major part in survival. Brian Lane's exceptional skills as both a fighter pilot and leader were obviously useless in such a role. He should have gone to a squadron operating wing sweeps. His experience would have been very useful in the summer of 1942 when we were having a difficult time with the advent of the FW 190.

David's story is a perfect example of real leadership. That Brian Lane should have gone to so much trouble on behalf of such a junior pilot is an example to anyone in a position of command; clearly he appreciated how strongly the young sergeant felt, and by rectifying the situation restored David Cox's faith in the RAF. Air Vice-Marshal Johnnie Johnson once said to me: 'You can learn the mechanics of leadership in the service, but true leadership is a gift, like that of a great painter or writer. You either have it or you don't.' There can be no doubt that Brian Lane had that gift. This is further evidenced by the fact that he would speak out for his pilots, the problems with 19 Squadron's cannon Spitfires being a prime example, even though the easiest course is never to 'rock the boat'. Wing Commander Peter Howard-Williams:

I well remember Brian Lane. When I left 19 Squadron to join 118 at Filton, he wrote 'Good Luck' above his final signature in my log book, which I have in front of me as I write this. He was a most pleasant man and very supportive at all times – he certainly stood up for his pilots.

I remember that he fitted two mirrors to the sides of his Spitfire and streamlined them in, to improve rearwards vision during combat. A wingless air commodore visited Duxford and told Brian to take them off. Brian apparently replied: 'Well you fly the bloody thing then!'

Personally I was shot at far more often than I shot at others during the war, and had a nasty cannon shell explode in my cockpit, just behind my seat, on one occasion; the armour plate saved me. Pilots like Brian Lane, however, were exceptional.

Wing Commander Frank Brinsden:

How pleased I am that Brian Lane is to receive public exposure and recognition at last. Being the commander of a squadron based on the fringe of the Battle of Britain area, he was prevented from showing his skills and therefore did not excite the acclaim afforded to commanders based in the southern counties.

Brian always used a silver cigarette case, but without affectation. He was always so much more sophisticated than the rest of us. His fine old black Armstrong Siddeley car was always highly polished, whereas our old Standards, Fords etc were battered and in need of loving care and attention.

Squadron Leader Brian Lane DFC was twenty-five years young when lost in 1942, and is remembered on panel 65 of the Runnymede Memorial. His final tally of victories was five enemy aircraft destroyed, three probables, one damaged and a share in an Me 110 destroyed.

Someone once said that in war there are no real victors; Oberleutnant Walter Leonhardt, who shot down and killed Squadron Leader Brian Lane on 13 December 1942, was himself reported missing over the North Sea just a few weeks later. This must surely illustrate how futile war is, and emphasize at what great cost to young life wars are fought, lost and won.

'Bunny' Currant pictured as a Flight Lieutenant after the Battle of Britain.

Flight Lieutenant Peter Brothers DFC of 32 Squadron, pictured at Hawkinge during the Battle of Britain.

During a combat over the Channel, Pilot Officer Rupert Smythe of 32 Squadron had a lucky escape when a German bullet ripped through his flying helmet. The Hurricane pilot escaped unscathed, and shows off his trophy to Flight Lieutenant Peter Brothers DFC back at Hawkinge.

A more dramatic angle on the classic photo, Flight Lieutenant Brothers third from right.

Opposite above: One of the classic photographs of 1940: Hurricane pilots of 32 Squadron at Hawkinge in July 1940; from left: P/Os R.F. Smythe, K.R. Gillman & E. Proctor, F/L P.M. Brothers DFC, P/Os D.H. Grice, P.M. Gardner DFC & A.F. Eckford. Situated on the coast near Folkestone, Hawkinge was the closest RAF station to the enemy – just twenty-two miles away across the Channel.

Opposite below: Reg Nutter while serving as a flying instructor in Canada.

Pilot Officer The Hon. David Coke.

Flight Lieutenant 'Cowboy' Blatchford.

Franek Surma pictured before the war at his niece's christening at Galkowice, Poland.

Sergeant Jack Stokoe, top button undone in true fighter pilot style, during the Battle of Britain.

Above: Brian Lane's wife, the pre-war racing driver Eileen Ellison, pictured with her Bugatti at Brooklands.

Left: Squadron Leader Stephenson's Spitfire, shot down on 26 May 1940, on the beach at Coquelles, near Calais.

Below left: Squadron Leader Brian Lane DFC.

Above: The South African Pilot Officer George Drake. Reported missing over Kent on 9 September 1940, the young pilot lay undiscovered with the wreckage of his Hurricane near Goudhurst until recovered by aviation archaeologists in 1972.

Right: Pilot Officer Harry Welford.

Squadron Leader Lane's Spitfire Mk IA at Fowlmere in September 1940.

Squadron Leader Brian Lane pictured at Fowlmere by a press photographer in September 1940.

Above: Squadron Leader Lane (centre) debriefs after a combat with Flight Lieutenant Walter 'Farmer' Lawson DFC (left) and Flight Sergeant George 'Grumpy' Unwin DFM.

Below: Lane and Lawson are joined at their airfield debrief by the Intelligence Officer and Sergeant Lloyd.

Hurricane P3021, in which Sergeant Bush crashed twice!

Sergeant 'Mike' Bush.

Sergeant Geoffrey Stevens.

Sergeant Stevens (right) with an unknown fellow NCO pilot during operational training.

Pilot Officer William Walker.

Above: While convalescing at the Palace Hotel, Torquay, Pilot Officer Walker, pictured here playing drums, and other officers formed a band to pass the time. The singer is Flight Lieutenant James Brindley Nicholson, the only fighter pilot to be awarded the Victoria Cross during World War Two.

Right: An X-ray of William Walker's ankle, showing Major Mölder's 7.9 mm bullet firmly lodged therein!

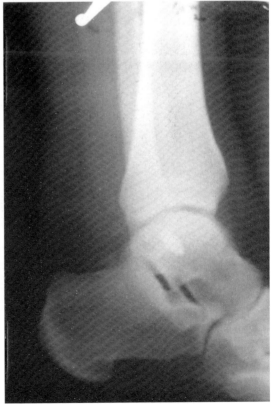

Above: The Hurricane-equipped 501 Squadron was in the line throughout the entire Battle of Britain, and unsurprisingly suffered the most casualties. These pilots of 501 are pictured at Kenley in September 1940; from left: Sgt T.G. Pickering, F/O D.A.E. Jones, F/O V.R. Snell, Sgt S.A.H. Whitehouse, unknown, Sgt R.J.K. Gent, F/S P.F. Morfill, next two unknown, P/O R.C. Dafforn and P/O S. Witorzenc (Polish). Both Gent and Dafforn lost their lives on active service during World War Two.

Left: Tony Pickering pictured while serving as a Flight Lieutenant in the Middle East.

Above: Sergeant Eddy Egan, a Volunteer Reservist flying Hurricanes with 501 Squadron. On patrol from Kenley on 17 September 1940, Sergeants Egan and Pickering were bounced by Me 109s; Egan was shot down and reported missing. His aircraft and remains were not found until 1976, when his aircraft and remains were recovered by aviation archaeologists from a wood near Bethersden, Kent. Sergeant Egan was subsequently buried with full military honours at Brookwood.

Below: During the Battle of Britain. Air Chief Marshal Dowding skilfully rotated his squadrons in and out of the combat zone; 501 Squadron, however, was in the front line throughout. Here a group of pilots from that squadron, operating from Gravesend, are seen at readiness in August 1940; from left: Sgts T.G. Pickering & R.J.K. Gent, F/S P.F. Morfill, Sgts P.C.P. Farnes, A. Glowacki (Polish), unknown, W.B. Henn, S.A.H. Whitehouse, J.H. Lacey & P/O R.C. Dafforn. Behind them is the Squadron Operations Caravan and two Hawker Hurricanes.

Above: Flight Sergeant George 'Grumpy' Unwin DFM and his Alsatian, 'Flash', pictured at Fowlmere during the Battle of Britain.

Below: 19 Squadron's pilots at Fowlmere during the Battle of Britain, adjacent to their temporary operations caravan and intelligence officer's tent. From left: S/L Brian Lane DFC (MIA 1942), Sgt J. Potter (POW 1940), Sgt B. Jennings DFM, F/S G. Unwin DFM, P/O R. Aeberhardt (KIA 1940), F/S H. Steere (KIA 1944), F/O F. Brinsden (POW 1944), F/L W. Lawson DFC (MIA 1941), P/O L.A. Haines DFC (Killed in a flying accident), F/L W. Clouston (POW 1942), & F/O H. Thomas.

Above: George Unwin teasing his beloved dog, 'Flash', at Fowlmere in 1940.

Below: George Unwin, pictured a few days before his death, aged ninety-three, in June 2006, proudly displaying a die-cast model of his Battle of Britain Spitfire.

Above: Sergeant David Cox.

Left: Pilot Officer Keith Lawrence DFC.

Above: Squadron Leader Douglas Bader (second right), and pilots of his 242 Squadron while away the hours of inactivity at Duxford. A man of action, it was Bader's exasperation at this situation that led to the controversial Duxford Wing during the Battle of Britain, led by Bader and in which David Cox flew frequently.

Right: Oberleutnant Gustav 'Mickey' Sprick.

Above: Pilot Officer Richard Jones.

Below: 64 Squadron outside the Officers' Mess at Kenley during the Battle of Britain; Pilot Officer Jones is fifth from right; the Squadron's highly respected and popular CO, Squadron Leader Don MacDonnell, the Laird of Glengarry, is seventh from right.

Sergeant Denis Nichols.

Pilot Officer Peter Down scrambles from North Weald in a 56 Squadron Hurricane during the Battle of Britain.

Opposite: Sergeant Peter Fox.

Peter Fox, left, meets eyewitnesses to his Battle of Britain crash in 1995.

Pre-Fighter Course, Montrose, June 1940. Sergeants Nichols and Wilkinson are at right, in that order, seated on bench, and Sergeant Fox is fourth from right, same row.

Opposite: Sergeant Ken Wilkinson, pictured at Fowlmere during the Battle of Britain.

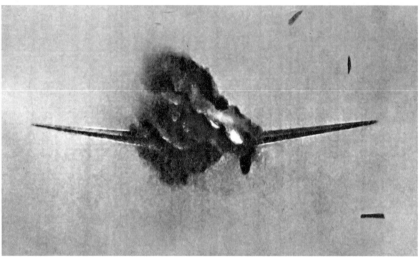

These pages: Rare camera footage of attacks on German aircraft from Spitfires and Hurricanes. The remains of two downed German aircraft.

Above: Oops! David Cox looks on while 'Farmer' Lawson recovers a homing pigeon, shot in error by 'Jock' Cunningham, with 12 bore in hand.

Opposite above: Pilot Officer Cunningham, left, at Readiness, Fowlmere, September 1940, with Sub-Lieutenant Giles 'Admiral' Blake (seated) and Flying Officer Frank Brinsden, a New Zealander.

Opposite below: Pilot Officer Wallace 'Jock' Cunningham DFC, pictured at Fowlmere during the Battle of Britain.

Squadron Leader Walter 'Farmer' Lawson DFC, reported missing over the North Sea during the same, futile, operation that saw 'Jock' Cunningham captured.

7

SERGEANT B.M. BUSH: 504 SQUADRON, HURRICANE PILOT

On 20 August 1939, Basil Martin 'Mike' Bush joined the RAFVR at Cambridge. From 1 September – 26 October he completed his 'square bashing' at 1 ITW, Cambridge, where he was billeted at St John's College. Thence he proceeded to 6 EFTS at Sywell, where he completed his *ab initio* instruction. After service flying training on Masters at Montrose, it was south to 7 OTU, Hawarden, to fly Harvards and 'Hurricanes at last!' On 16 July, 1940, Sergeant Bush was posted to 504 'City of Nottingham' Squadron, a Hurricane squadron of the AAF. He joined the Squadron at Castletown in Scotland, and flew south to Hendon with the unit on 5 September.

Awaiting the call to scramble, Mike recalled that appropriately the pilots' favourite tune was Vera Lynn's 'Room Five Hundred & Four'. On 7 September, 504 was among the squadrons scrambled in response to the major attack on London. Over the Thames Estuary, Mike's Hurricane, P3021, TM-N, was shot up by a 109. A cannon shell passed through his instrument panel and into the reserve petrol tank beyond:

I was damned lucky not to catch fire as when hit the petrol splashed all over me! Fortunately it did not ignite and I managed a safe forced-landing on the Isle of Sheppey. It was a bit hairy for a moment or two, though! Due to repairs being carried out I was unable to return to Hendon with my aircraft until September 9th. They gave me a week off to recover, so I did not fly again until September 17th.

On 25 September, the Luftwaffe mounted a successful raid on the Bristol Aircraft Company at Filton, near Bristol. As there were several other important targets in the West Country connected with the aircraft industry, and in anticipation of further attacks, the decision was made to move 504 Squadron from Hendon to Filton. The Squadron moved there the following day, which proved a wise move as on 27 September, the Germans returned. On that occasion the target was Parnall Aircraft at Yate, only this time the enemy was harshly treated by 10 Group's squadrons, including 504. On 30 September, KG 55 intended to smash Westland Aircraft at Yeovil but due to cloud covering the target bombed the neighbouring town of Sherborne by mistake. In what was the last truly great daylight battle of 1940, 504's Hurricanes were scrambled from Filton and pursued the retreating Heinkels until dangerously close to the Cherbourg peninsula. Sergeant Jones shot down two He 111s, and Sergeant Bush damaged another, as did several other pilots:

After the interception I was unable to make radio contact with Filton. As it was getting dark and I was lost somewhere south of Bristol I was fearful of getting caught up in balloon cables, so I decided to land in a field. I picked what I thought to be a long landing run in a particular field which I had spotted, but on the approach I came in low over a hedge and landed, only to discover that it was a much shorter field than the one I had selected and saw a brick wall ahead! Having touched down I could do nothing else but jam on my brakes and switch off the engine. This resulted in tipping the Hurricane up onto its nose. It then flipped over onto its back and I was left hanging by my harness upside down and several feet from the ground. Thankfully I was soon rescued by Observer Corps personnel from nearby Priddy village. By coincidence, the aircraft concerned was P3021, in which I had been shot down over the Thames.

At that juncture, P3021 and Mike Bush parted company, as the aircraft was taken away to a repair depot. The Hurricane was to have further adventures with other pilots before finally crashing and being written off over a year later.

On 17 December 1941, 504 Squadron moved from Filton to Exeter, also in 10 Group, where it was joined later by the Spitfires of 66 Squadron. During that period, Mike often flew nocturnal patrols:

We were sent up to take over from the AA at Plymouth during a raid on February 10th, 1941. The guns were supposed to stop firing and let us have a go, but they kept on, apparently uncaring as to who got hit. We soon got fed up with this and returned to base, however!

Mike was commissioned later that year, and went to fly Hurricanes in Russia. After that tour he became an instructor prior to converting

Mosquito bombers. Flying with 139 Squadron at Upwood, Mike flew fifty-four operational trips, eighteen of which were to Berlin, the 'Big City', itself. A tour was actually considered complete at thirty trips, so Mike's DFC was clearly much deserved.

After the war, Mike returned to banking and eventually retired with his wife, Irene, to a tranquil spot in Lincolnshire. Although a member of the Battle of Britain Fighter Association, Flight Lieutenant B.M. 'Mike' Bush DFC has all but faded into obscurity. 'I was just doing my job, along with countless others. I certainly do not consider that I did anything special, far from it.'

Typically modest, Mike Bush was a real gentleman, and is sadly one of the Few no longer with us.

8

SERGEANT G. STEVENS: 151/213 SQUADRONS, HURRICANE PILOT

Geoffrey Stevens was another VR pilot called to full-time service on 1 September 1939. The twenty-two-year-old completed his flying training and learned to fly Hurricanes at 6 OTU in July 1940. The following month saw him posted to 151 Squadron at North Weald, but having been engaged throughout the Battle of France and the struggle for Britain to date, the unit was rested soon after. Sergeant Stevens courageously volunteered to remain in the combat area, and was posted to 213 Squadron.

At 1610 hours on 30 September 1940, Squadron Leader Duncan MacDonald's 213 Squadron was scrambled from Tangmere, the famous Sector Station on the south coast. The Hurricanes were initially vectored to intercept a raid of 200 plus bandits that had crossed the coast two minutes previously. Geoffrey recalls an unexpected turn of events:

Quite abruptly and without warning we were ordered to turn 180° and told 'Buster' (travel at full throttle, make all haste). R/T talk between our 'Bearskin Leader' and Control elicited the information that it was a 60 plus raid (returning from an attack on Yeovil). We soon saw the enemy, first as dots that gradually developed into a mixture of He 111s and Me 110s, and some Me 109s that were, as usual, above us. We were at about the same height as the bombers and 110s. I initially went for one of the latter, but he evaded by executing a spiral dive. I did not follow as I wished to retain height, but then saw a formation of three He 111s below me, so I dived on them, selecting the left-hand aircraft as my target. I got a fair amount of stick from all three gunners and opened with quite a long burst. However, I was travelling too fast and broke away left and downwards. I pulled back into a steep, almost vertical climb at full throttle, intending to come around again for another go, feeling quite sure that I had silenced the gunner in the aircraft I had fired at. At this point, near the top of the climb, the belly of an Me 110 slid into view, going from right to left. I opened up and continued climbing. I saw strikes all along the underside, but I had reached the point of stall and at that moment ran out of ammunition. I fell out of the skies, as the saying goes, and as there was no point in returning to the fray I let the aircraft dive. This was very nearly my undoing as I had built up too much speed and had great difficulty in getting out of the dive. The airscrew over-revved and sprayed oil all over the windscreen but thankfully I made it by about 100 feet. Later, the airframe fitter told me that several wooden slats which ran underside and aft of the cockpit had been stoved in by my pull out.

In this particular engagement, 213 had met the enemy at about 1700 hours over Portland. For no loss, Squadron Leader Macdonald and Flying Officer Kellow each destroyed an Me 110, while Sub-Lieutenant Jeram, a FAA pilot seconded to Fighter Command, probably destroyed another. Sergeants Stevens and Barrow both claimed 110s as damaged, and Pilot Officer Atkinson destroyed a 109. As 213 broke away, Squadron Leader John Sample's 504 Squadron hit the raiders, south of Portland, and so the battle continued to rage. On 17 October, Geoffrey was in trouble again, as he recalled for me many years later:

We of 213 Squadron were scrambled late in the afternoon, getting on for 1700 hours, and as we climbed away from Tangmere I remember thinking that I wished Flight Lieutenant Jackie Sing (commander of 'A' Flight) was leading us, as in my opinion he was the best. Neither did we have a tail end Charlie, for reasons that escaped me.

We climbed to about 17,000 feet when I noticed anti-aircraft shells bursting ahead and below. I reported this and at about the same time we had a course correction starboard. As we turned I saw strikes on Red Two, just ahead of me. We were flying the stupid close formation 'vic' of three aircraft in line astern (I was Yellow 2). Simultaneously I was hit in the engine by three or four cannon shells. The rev counter went off the clock and smoke and flames enveloped the outside. The standard practice if hit was to get out of the action as quickly as one could. I therefore shoved the stick over and went into a spiral dive. Flames, smoke and glycol fumes were everywhere, and I went down switching off everything I could think of.

I entered cloud at about 10,000 feet, coming out at 5,000 feet whilst preparing to bale out. The flames appeared to have stopped. I lifted up my goggles to have a look round and saw that I was over a town. I knew that if I baled out my aircraft would cause some severe damage, possibly loss of life. A field containing an AA gun was within gliding distance and so I opted for a forced-landing.

I did not appear to be in any immediate danger at this stage and so settled into a straight glide towards the field. Having sorted everything out in my mind, knowing exactly what I was going to do, I was dismayed to see what I have since described as electric light bulbs, but what was actually tracer, going past my cockpit. Looking in my rear view mirror I saw a yellow nosed 109 on my tail. Without power, evasive action is limited, especially with so little height to play with. I used rudder to skid out of the German's sights, and am told that fortunately he'd been chased off by another Hurricane. I had lost height, however.

The effect of this on my carefully planned approach was disastrous. I opened the hood and blinded myself with glycol fumes. I put my goggles on again, but by this time I was very low, about 100 feet, travelling much too fast and in the wrong position for an approach to the field. Everything was wrong! I did a steep left-handed turn towards the field and slammed the Hurricane onto the ground, it was all I could do. It was unfortunate that I had been forced to choose the one approach that ended up with my wing root against a four feet thick tree stump. The aircraft shot into the air and over onto its back, into a sort of marsh. With all that had gone on leading up to this, I had omitted to lock the sliding cockpit hood open, and my harness back. The hood consequently slammed shut and I was propelled forward upon impact with some force, cutting my head on the reflector gunsight.

I was now hanging upside down with blood running down my face. I could smell the petrol leaking out everywhere and hear the hissing of the cooling engine in the wet marsh. Otherwise everything seemed dead quiet. I tried to open the hood but it was useless. I was expecting the aircraft to go up in flames at any time and seemed powerless to effect an escape. I carefully released my straps and let myself down so that I lay on my back on top of the cockpit hood. I think that this was more to do *something* than continue hanging upside down doing nowt!

Although it seemed like an age, assistance actually came very quickly. People seemed to come from nowhere, including the Army. One helpful farmer got himself a corner post with a pointed metal end and rammed it through the Perspex hood. Had I still been hanging upside down it would have gone straight through my head, as it was it went just past my nose! To cut a long story short, one wing was lifted enough to allow the hood to slide back. The small clearance from the ground was sufficient for me, I was out of the wrecked Hurricane like a bullet from a gun! I'd never moved so fast in my life!

When I got out I could not stand up because the stick had come back and whacked my knee and I was somewhat shaken. However, with two men supporting me on each arm we made it to HQ and I remember being amazed at the number of people there. As we walked up the field it was a crescent of people all looking to the centre. I only mention this because shaken though I was it left a clear impression that I can remember to this day. They took me to Ashford Hospital, and later the soldiers returned and invited me to join them for a drink that night. Although I was willing the doctor was having none of it!

It is believed that 213 Squadron had clashed with Me 109s of JG 77, flying out of Marquise, which were engaged on a Freie Hunt.

In a classic example of over-claiming caused by the confusion created by a large number of fleeting fighters, seven 109 pilots claimed to have destroyed Hurricanes. In fact, only three were lost. It is possible that Geoffrey Stevens was shot down by Gefrieter Karl Raisinger of 3/JG 77. Just eight days later, Raisinger's 109 was hit in both the engine and radiator by an RAF fighter, forcing him to crash land near Saltdean. Although safe, the young German was captured and spent the rest of a long war in captivity.

Geoffrey Stevens remained in the post war RAF as a controller, but has passed away since recording his Battle of Britain story.

9

PILOT OFFICER W.L.B. WALKER: 616 SQUADRON, SPITFIRE PILOT

William Walker joined the RAFVR in 1938, while working for Halls Oxford Brewery and undertaking flying lessons at Kidlington. When called up on 1 September 1939, Sergeant Walker had completed sufficient flying hours for his elementary training to be considered complete. He therefore went straight to ITW Cambridge, and afterwards to Brize Norton where he was converted to Harvards. There, however, William had the most incredible escape when he walked away, virtually unscathed, from an absolutely horrendous night landing accident. Indeed, having staggered from the crash site across several fields, when he walked into the Mess his fellow students assumed that they were looking at a ghost! As William later said:

> Whilst at Kidlington they had 26 student pilots, and I was No. 26. My instructor said that being twice 13 it was a lucky number; having escaped the Harvard crash I was inclined to agree!

In April 1940, William received not only his coveted pilot's flying brevet but also a commission. On 18 June, he joined 616 'South Yorkshire' Squadron of the AAF, based at Leconfield:

The early days of war were interesting in so far as we were so unprepared for what was to come. It is my lasting regret that I did not have more operational training – trying to pick it up with the Squadron straight from flying school was a pretty haphazard affair. For instance, I flew my first Spitfire on June 23rd, and was declared operational on July 1st.

Flying from Leconfield, 616 Squadron was involved in the 'Junkers Party', the action fought off the north-east coast on 15 August. On that occasion the Germans had not expected to find Spitfires and Hurricanes so far north, wrongly believing that all available single-engine fighters must have already been committed to battle in the south. From the aerodromes in Norway from whence these raiders came, England lay beyond the range of the Me 109, so consequently escort was provided by Me 110s. The latter proved inadequate to the task, however, and the Germans took a beating, so much so, in fact, that the Luftwaffe never again tried to attack the north in daylight. 616 Squadron engaged fifty bombers and a gaggle of 110s at 15,000 feet, ten miles off Flamborough Head. Subsequently, eight bombers were claimed as destroyed, four probably destroyed and two damaged, all for no loss. The absence of Me 109s, however, gave the inexperienced defenders a false impression of air fighting. This was soon to change, drastically.

On 19 August, 616 Squadron flew south to Kenley Sector Station, in 11 Group. Only the previous day, Kenley had been hit hard, and so the Station bore little resemblance to the formal and orderly environment left behind by 616 at Leconfield, as William remembers:

The Mess at Kenley was a rather sombre building and far removed from the modern, light and cheerful Mess at Leconfield. Kenley bore many scars as witness to damage and loss of life caused by enemy action. An atmosphere of purpose prevailed and we found ourselves having to respond to a life of far greater activity than at Leconfield where only a few minor raids had disrupted our existence.

Three days later the Squadron experienced its first clash with the enemy while operating from Kenley: Green Section was bounced over Dover by a Staffel of JG 51's Me 109s. Within seconds Pilot Officer Hugh 'Cocky' Dundas was taking to his parachute, his Spitfire in flames, and a cannon shell damaged Pilot Officer Lionel 'Buck' Casson's fighter. Sergeant Wareing, however, claimed a 109 destroyed in the resulting skirmish.

On 25 August, 616 Squadron was vectored to intercept a raid comprising twenty Do 17s escorted by a Gruppe of Me 109s. Before reaching the bombers, the Spitfires were bounced and broken up by the 109s. Sergeant Westmoreland was killed and Sergeant Wareing was 'Missing' (later reported as a prisoner). In response, the Auxiliaries claimed two enemy aircraft destroyed and a probable. William Walker:

> We were very unsure of ourselves at this time. Everything happened so quick, and of course our formations of vics and lines astern were all wrong. There was so little information available to us. Very little was passed on by those squadrons that were relieved as they just couldn't wait to get the hell out of the place! Fighting in the south, where the 109s always seemed to have the advantage of height and sun, was very different indeed to chasing after unescorted bombers up north.

That having been said, 616 Squadron's initiation was not as brutal as experienced by some unfortunate squadrons. Studying the casualty lists, every now and again a squadron suddenly appears and suffers a far greater number of losses than the average. Inevitably, if one delves a little deeper, this invariably occurred when the squadron in question met Me 109s in strength for the first time. The period of adjustment to the infinitely fiercer tempo of combat can, therefore, only be described as traumatic. 26 August 1940, is a day that William Walker will always remember:

It was still dark when the Orderly awoke me with a cup of tea at 0330 that morning, just two days after my 27th birthday, which had passed unnoticed amid the current level of activity and excitement. I drank my tea slowly and gradually awakened to another day. It seemed such a short while since we had been 'stood down' the previous evening at about 2100 hours, and after which a few beers refreshed our spirits before bed. However, I dressed and went down to breakfast, always a quiescent occasion at the unearthly hour of 0400! The sound of aero engines could be heard in the distance, indicating that the groundcrews were already busy. One was so accustomed to the drone of engines that it passed almost unnoticed amid the clatter of cups and plates.

Following breakfast I joined other pilots outside the Mess. We all climbed aboard a lorry and were driven to dispersal, to remain at 'Readiness', where a hut and a few tents constituted the Squadron's base. A few days earlier the Duke of Kent had actually paid us a visit at our modest location to wish us well.

That day I was allocated Spitfire R6633, and was to fly in Yellow Section led by Flying Officer Teddy St Aubyn, a former Guards officer. The plane stood within 50 yards of our hut and so I walked over and placed my parachute in the cockpit with the straps spread apart and ready for wearing immediately I jumped in. Two of the groundcrew stood by the plane with the starter battery plugged in. I walked back to the hut as the sun rose and added a little warmth to a chilly start. Pilots sat about either reading or exchanging the usual banter that had become routine. We had spent many months in this way, which was now a way of life. At 8 a.m. our second breakfast arrived at dispersal, and was just as fulfilling as our breakfast of four hours earlier: coffee, eggs, bacon, sausages and toast to replenish our undiminished appetites.

The telephone suddenly rang in the dispersal hut, and a shout went up of 'Yellow Section Scramble! Patrol Dungeness/Dover Angels 20!' This sent me running for my Spitfire. I leapt on to the wing and was in the cockpit, parachute strapped on, within seconds. I pressed the starter and the engine fired immediately. The groundcrew removed the plug from the cowling and pulled the remote starter battery clear. I waved the chocks away and taxied the aircraft, following my Section Leader and Sergeant Ridley to the end of the runway for take off. Within minutes, Yellow Section was airborne. We headed east, climbing quickly and passing through cloud, reached our patrol course in some 15–20 minutes. We flew in a wide formation that day, in fact, and had been airborne for about an hour without sighting an enemy aircraft when suddenly several Me 109s appeared.

High above and unseen by Yellow Section, however, was the entire JG 51 (about 100 Me 109s), led in person by the Kommodore, Major Werner Mölders (the so-called 'Father of Modern Air Fighting' himself) on a geschwader strength freie hunt. Dropping behind and below the Spitfires, Mölders selected William Walker's Spitfire and attacked from the blind spot:

When the 109s hit us I banked sharply to port, towards a 109, but suddenly my machine was raked with bullets. The one that attacked me did so from below and behind, I never even saw it. The flying controls ceased to respond and a sudden pain in my leg indicated that I had been hit. Baling out seemed to be a sensible option. My two comrades, St Aubyn and Ridley, had both vanished.

I pulled back the hood and tried to stand up but realised that I had not disconnected the radio lead, which was still plugged in, and had to remove my helmet before I was free to jump. The aircraft was still banking to port, so jumping out was easy, I was still at 20,000 feet and pulled the ripcord immediately. A sudden jerk indicated that all was well and that I was on my way down. I looked around but could not see a single aircraft. Below there was 10/10ths cloud. I had no idea where I was. It seemed to take ages to reach the clouds and passing through I realised that I was still over the Channel. Thinking that I would soon land in the sea prompted the thought that I had better remove my heavy flying boots. I did this and let them fall. I watched them spiral down for what seemed like ages and then realised that I was much higher than I thought. I inflated my Mae West and eventually landed in the sea. I easily discarded my parachute and could see the wreck of a ship sticking out of the water a few hundred yards away and swam to it. I reached it and climbed on, sitting there for about half an hour until a fishing boat came alongside and I clambered aboard. I was now extremely cold from my immersion and wet clothes.

The fishermen gave me a cup of tea, well laced with whisky, as we headed for land. When about two miles offshore, an RAF launch came alongside and I was transferred to it. By this time the tea concoction had worked quite disastrously on my cold stomach. Fortunately there was a loo aboard to which I retired with some relief. I was still enthroned when we reached Ramsgate harbour. An aircraftman kept knocking on the door and enquiring whether I was all right. It was some time before I was able to emerge! I as carried up the steps to a waiting ambulance, by which time quite a crowd had gathered and gave me a cheer as I was put in the ambulance. A kind old lady handed me a packet of cigarettes, so I decided that being shot down was perhaps not such a bad thing after all!

Yellow Section's Sergeant Marmaduke Ridley had not been so lucky, however: he was dead, having been shot down by Hauptmann 'Joschko' Fözoe, Staffelkapitän of 4/JG 51. Yellow One, Flying Officer St Aubyn, had been shot down by Oberleutnant 'Pips' Priller, Staffelkapitän of 6/JG 51. The Spitfire caught fire but the wounded pilot managed to crash-land at Eastchurch. 616 Squadron also suffered other losses, including the death of Pilot Officer Moberley and another pilot wounded. William Walker summarizes the day's events as 'traumatic'. More accurately for the Squadron as a whole, they could be described as 'catastrophic'. Since having arrived at Kenley a week previously, seven Spitfires lost, four pilots wounded and four killed; the squadron's clerk, clearly a master of the understatement, had recorded the action as 'a very unfortunate engagement'. The following day, while in transit between Ramsgate Hospital and RAF Hospital Halton, William Walker stopped off at Kenley to collect his belongings:

Whilst there I asked my driver to take me to dispersal so that I could say farewell to any remaining pilots. It proved a sad occasion, however, as the squadron had suffered severe losses and very few pilots actually remained operational.

It was almost 2200 hours when we arrived at Halton RAF Hospital, where I was put to bed. Unfortunately, by this late hour, the kitchens had been closed for some hours but a wonderful night nurse produced an equally wonderful and indeed appropriate meal: scrambled eggs!

After breakfast the following morning, doctors appeared and attended to the officers in my large ward of some 20 beds. Nobody came to see me, however, and apart from getting rather painful, I was beginning to worry about gangrene. The previous 48 hours had been somewhat traumatic to say the least, so my concern was not entirely unjustified!

At noon the head doctor, a group captain, did his rounds. As he passed my bed he asked what I was in for. I told him that I had a bullet in my leg. He said 'Oh yes, and who is looking after you?' When I told him that I had yet to see a doctor despite having arrived the previous night I thought that he was going to have a convulsion! He literally exploded and his wrath remains a vivid memory. Never were so many doctors torn off a bigger strip. It was action stations from then on, and within just 10 minutes I was in the operating theatre.

When I regained consciousness, the surgeon was by my bedside. He said 'I think you may like to have this,' and handed me an armour-piercing bullet. He then told me that as he was prising open the bone in my leg to extract the bullet it shot out and hit the ceiling of the operating theatre! I still possess it today as a cherished souvenir.

Fortunately my sense of humour never quite left me, and when a doctor later asked how my accident happened I assured him that I was not the victim of an accident, but of a determined attempt on my life by a German fighter pilot!

On 26 August, 616 Squadron had lost seven of the twelve Spitfires flown on operations that day; two pilots were dead and four more wounded. William Walker was one of the lucky ones.

On 3 September, 616 Squadron, comprising just eight of its original members who arrived at Kenley on 19 August, was relieved at Kenley by 64 Squadron. In those fifteen days, 616 had lost a total of eleven Spitfires destroyed and three damaged. Five pilots had been killed, six wounded and one captured. In response, the Squadron claimed the destruction of ten enemy aircraft destroyed, three probably destroyed, and six damaged. Of this 'bag', seven destroyed, two probables and three damaged were claimed by one man: Flight Lieutenant Denys Gillam AFC. For this feat he later received recognition by way of a DFC.

William Walker, his leg in plaster, was sent to complete his treatment at the Palace Hotel, Torquay, which had been converted into an RAF Hospital. Another patient there at the time was Flight Lieutenant James Brindley Nicholson, as William remembers:

A telegram arrived for him. Nick's response was simply 'Well, what d'you make of that?' He was genuinely puzzled, and not a little embarrassed, that of hundreds of brave deeds performed by RAF fighter pilots that summer, his had been singled out for this very great honour. His was the only Fighter Command VC because due to the speed of fighter combat it is difficult to find witnesses, supporting evidence being a pre-requisite. At first 'Nick' got into trouble for being improperly dressed because he refused to stitch the maroon ribbon onto his tunic. In the end I think he adopted the attitude that he was accepting the medal on behalf of us all. He was a good sport, in fact, and we enjoyed playing together in a four-piece band that we formed with other wounded pilots down at Torquay.

On May 1st, 1941, I was considered fit enough to return to operations, so I re-joined 616 Squadron, which was then a part of Wing Commander Douglas Bader's Wing at Tangmere and was much changed. When I reported to the Wing Leader he tore me off a strip for being so careless as to have been shot down, which I thought was a bit off, to say the least. Suffice to say that I did not take to him, and he not to me, so three weeks later I was posted to an Aircraft Delivery Flight at Hendon. Later that summer, of course, it was announced that Douglas Bader himself had been shot down and captured by the Germans!

The rest of William's war was 'enjoyable but mundane', but on 8 May 1945, he was able to call himself a survivor:

Looking back after all these years to the time when so many of us on Course 45 had such high hopes and felt invulnerable, it is terribly sad that some would not survive the year, would never even see the enemy, all of their hard work and training proving fruitless. Whilst they were just casualty statistics in the official records, to me they are a reminder of many happy days of friendship that are still well worth recalling and should be remembered.

They were the most exhilarating days, but one lost so many friends who were all so young. It is sad that the best pilots seemed to get killed whilst the 'hams' like me survived.

10

SERGEANT T.G. PICKERING: 501 SQUADRON, HURRICANE PILOT

Tony Garforth Pickering was an RAFVR pilot who had joined on 30 July 1939, and learned to fly at Ansty. When the country mobilized for war, Tony was called up immediately and after an initial period at 3 ITW at Hastings, commenced his service flying training. Upon completion, he did not go to an OTU but was posted straight from flying Harvard trainers to a fighter squadron:

I was a Sergeant Pilot during the Battle of Britain. First I was posted to 32 Squadron but had never flown a Hurricane. The CO sent me and some others to an OTU to learn how. We returned to be told that the squadron was moving north for a rest, but, as we didn't need one, we would be posted to 501 'County of Gloucester' Squadron, an auxiliary unit which was flying Hurricanes at Kenley. The ace 'Ginger' Lacey was also an NCO pilot with 501 at the time.

I was flying with Sergeant Eddie Egan when he was killed. I did not know Eddie terribly well but I suppose he was my friend and he was a nice lad, he really was. We were flying along, just the two of us, looking about all the time for trouble, and I saw four Spitfires behind us. We were talking to each other on the R/T, monitoring the movements of the 'Spitfires'. Suddenly one of them zoomed forward, just left the others standing, and shot Eddie down. I turned towards his assailant but the old Hurricane was just too slow, the Hun just shot Eddie and flew off with the others, they just climbed high and left us. I looked over the side and saw Eddie going down, the aircraft in flames. Eddie went in in a wood outside Ashford in Kent. After I landed I filed a report on the incident, giving the location of where Eddie had crashed. Six months later I had to see the Air Ministry and pin-point the site as Eddie had never been found. The next I ever heard of Eddie Egan was when I happened to read an article in the Sunday Express a few years ago in which it said that Eddie's bones had been discovered by an aviation archaeology group at the very spot that I had advised the Air Ministry that he had crashed all those years ago. I got in touch with them and told them what I knew, and through them contacted Eddie's sister, a very nice lady whom I still see occasionally. There was an inquest but I was amazed not to be called as a witness, I did see him go in after all! Incidentally, the plane that shot Eddie down did not look like an Me 109. We thought that they were 'He 113s' at the time, but we now know that the type was merely a propaganda ruse by the Germans. The Hun involved definitely had elliptical wings.

I was shot down on September 11th, 1940, in Hurricane P5200, SD-W. The CO, Squadron Leader Hogan, had ordered us to perform a head-on attack on a large formation of German bombers heading for London, I cannot recall whether they were Dorniers or Heinkels, but they were definitely not Ju 88s. Anyway, we dived head-on at the Huns and I pressed the gun button and shut my eyes! One of the nose gunners gave me a squirt and hit the sump. I started smoking and managed to spiral down away from the fight. It was a lovely day and I could see Kenley below quite clearly. As there was no-one about I thought that I could just come down quite slowly and make a nice landing. At about 3,000 feet the petrol caught fire and I was over the side pretty sharpish! The Hurricane went down and crashed and I landed in a guards depot where I was given a couple of whiskies. I was wearing ordinary uniform trousers, shoes, an open neck shirt with no tie as it was hot, and that was it. I hadn't had a shave that morning and I remember being a bit singed about the face and hair but was otherwise uninjured.

Another time I came across a lone Ju 88 somewhere over Kent, heading back to sea. I thought it would be no problem to catch up the Hun, press the button and that would be it. I slotted in behind and ran flat out to catch him. Suddenly he just pulled away from me, just left me standing, had at least an extra 50 m.p.h on me, and that was the last that I saw of him. The Hurricane just wasn't fast enough, we even used to bend the throttle levers in flight trying to squeeze a bit more boost out of the Merlin. A Spitfire would have caught that Ju 88. In the Hurricane's favour was that it could take a terrific amount of punishment, the Spitfire not quite as much.

I was 18 during the Battle of Britain. I came from a small village where everyone knew everyone else, we went to school, did our homework in the evenings and went to church on Sundays. We were innocents, really, the RAF was a bit of a shock, all these chaps who were going around night clubs and girls, it was something to touch a girl's arm at a dance then, not like it is now!

Tony Picketing was lucky to survive the Battle of Britain. 501 Squadron was in the front line throughout the entire sixteen week battle and suffered the highest number of pilots killed by any fighter squadron during that time – nineteen. He later left behind the lumbering Hurricane and, having been commissioned in December 1941, became a flight commander on 113 Squadron with which he served until January 1944. A year later he was posted overseas and commanded the Bombing and Gunnery School at El Ballah before leaving the RAF in December 1945. One of the youngest of the surviving Few, Tony Pickering is now a frequent guest at events promoting interest in the summer of 1940, and long may that remain the case.

11

FLIGHT SERGEANT G.C. UNWIN: 19 SQUADRON, SPITFIRE PILOT

George Unwin will always be remembered as having been among Fighter Command's most outstanding pilots in 1940. A Yorkshireman, George was the son of a miner and was a grammar school boy. In 1929, he joined the RAF as an apprentice clerk, but volunteered for aircrew in 1935. Selected for pilot training, he began learning to fly at Woodley before completing his service flying training at Wittering. He then joined 19 Squadron at Duxford.

At this time, 19 Squadron was equipped with the Gauntlet biplane fighter, but in August 1938 became the first squadron to receive the new Supermarine Spitfire. George Unwin was, in fact, the first RAF NCO pilot to ever fly a Spitfire. On 9 March 1939, however, he found himself in trouble during a training flight in K9797:

A coolant pipe had broken causing the engine to partially seize up. I decided to land on a large playing field, near Sudbury in Essex, and was doing fine, with undercarriage down, until the school children who were playing on the various pitches saw me descending (I was apparently on fire and trailing smoke). They ran towards me and on to the path I had selected for a landing. I was then less than 100 feet, so decided to stuff the Spitfire into the thick hawthorn hedge just in front of me. The impact broke my straps, and I gashed my right eyebrow on the windscreen but was otherwise unhurt. For this I received an Air Officer Commanding's commendation.

By September 1939, 19 Squadron was the most experienced Spitfire squadron in the RAF. In February the following year, the unit was joined by Flying Officer Douglas Bader who had lost both legs in a flying accident during 1931. Before then he had been a gifted sportsman and aerobatics pilot who had been a Cranwell chum of the Commanding Officer's, Squadron Leader Geoffrey Stephens. Regulations, however, prevented Bader from flying before the war, after he had mastered his artificial limbs and in spite of passing the necessary flying test. As a result he left the service in 1933, but upon declaration of war, as a trained pilot, was welcomed back into the fold. Much had changed during the time that he had been away, however, not least the aircraft. In Bader's pre-war days he had flown Bristol Bulldog biplane fighters with a fixed pitch propeller and fixed undercarriage. Now he was learning to fly the fast Spitfire monoplane, the airscrew of which (Mk IA) had a two-pitch setting, and retractable undercarriage. Changing pitch is similar to the effect of changing gear in a car, but on one occasion Bader attempted to take off in the wrong pitch, the result of which was him barely coming 'unstuck' and crashing into a dry stone wall! Ironically, his artificial legs were damaged beyond repair and so he received a replacement pair, as George remembers:

Sometime after Bader's accident we were at Horsham St Faith's, to which we flew from Duxford every morning to be at Readiness for convoy patrols and the like. Whilst slumbering in the pilot's hut early one morning, Bader persisted in filing his new tin legs, to get them in perfect working order and fit, and so I remonstrated with him for this constant scratching and scraping whilst I was trying to sleep. At the time, the Walt Disney film 'Snow White & the Seven Dwarves' was very popular, and Bader replied 'Oh shut up, Grumpy!', 'Grumpy' being one of the characters in the film. The name stuck, and from then on 'Grumpy' has been my nickname!

When the fighting started on the Continent in May 1940, Air Chief Marshal Dowding refused to send his precious Spitfires over the Channel. The Advanced Air Striking Force, already in France, was equipped with Hurricanes, which were more plentiful although slightly lacking in performance. As losses mounted, Hurricane squadrons flew from coastal bases like Hawkinge to operate in France on a daily basis. Every night they flew back to England, however, and so it went on. The Spitfire pilots were frustrated, but their Commander-in-Chief knew that if France fell, the Germans were likely to attack Britain with a view to mounting a seaborne invasion, and that being the case he would need all of his fighters, and Spitfires in particular, to defend these shores. To Air Chief Marshal Dowding, 'security of base' was the most important doctrine. At the time of Dunkirk, Spitfires did participate in the air operation in support of the evacuation. Although they operated little further than the French coast, for the first time the Spitfire clashed with the Me 109.

On 26 May 1940, 19 Squadron experienced its first major combat of the war. Over Calais, Squadron Leader Stephenson led his Spitfires in a textbook formation attack on a group of Stukas. Flying along sedately, their speed matching that of their prey, the Spitfires made an easy target for the marauding and combat experienced Me 109s, which fell on 19 Squadron in a surprise attack. Within seconds two Spitfires were despatched from the fight: Squadron Leader Stephenson forced-landed on the nearby beach and was captured, and Pilot Officer Watson was killed. In a flash, the 109s were gone, leaving the Spitfire pilots shaken and confused. George Unwin:

> The tacticians who wrote the book really believed that in the event of war it would be fighter versus bomber only. What they could not foresee was Hitler's modern ground tactics that would take his armies to the Channel ports in an unprecedented advance, thus providing bases for his fighters in the Pas-de-Calais and therefore putting London itself within their limited range. Our tight formations, which we practised extensively before the war, were actually useless in combat, what happened to Stephenson and Watson being a perfect example of just how flawed our fighter tactics were. Over Dunkirk, we had tried to put into practice years of peacetime training, based upon unrealistic perceptions, and paid a heavy price. Our formation attacks were perfectly impressive for the Hendon Air Pageant, but useless for modern air fighting which, after all, is for what they were intended.

The Spitfire squadrons had to learn fast, on the job, and indeed they did. By the end of Operation DYNAMO, Flight Sergeant

Unwin had personally destroyed three enemy aircraft, plus a probable and a share in a probable He 111.

When the Battle of Britain started, so too began a frustrating time for the pilots of 12 Group, whose role was to defend the industrial Midlands and the north. The enemy's main thrust was against London and the south-east, and targets along the south coast generally. These areas, however, were defended by 11 and 10 Groups. The Air-Officer-Commanding of 11 Group, Air Vice-Marshal Keith Park, understood perfectly the System and knew what was required of him. So as to preserve his fighters, he attacked using penny packet formations, as a result of which his pilots were always outnumbered. When 11 Group's airfields were threatened, however, and when his own fighters were in action further forward, Air Vice-Marshal Park was entitled to call upon both 10 and 12 Groups to protect them. As we have already read previously in this book, for certain 12 Group personalities, including both the AOC and Acting Squadron Leader Douglas Bader, the CO of 242 Squadron, this lack of direct involvement was intolerable.

By mid-August, in spite of the heavy activity in the south-east, 19 Squadron remained engaged upon providing protection to convoys moving along Britain's east coast. At 1730 hours on 16 August, however, 'A' Flight, which was returning to Coltishall from such a patrol, was asked to investigate an incoming raid. George recalls the incident well:

We left Coltishall at 1715 and were ordered to 15,000 feet, which was altered to 12,000. After 20 minutes a large formation of enemy aircraft was spotted, bombers escorted by Me 110s at the rear and

Me 109s above. As we went in to attack the bombers, the 110s saw us and attacked. I latched on to a 110 and gave him a short burst. He half-rolled and went down almost vertically. I could not see what had happened to him as I was attacked by another. I out-turned him and found myself with a perfect target at close range. My starboard cannon had a stoppage, but I fired the remainder of my port cannon's ammunition into the 110. Bits fell off the enemy aircraft and he went into a steep dive, during which the tail came off. I followed him down and when I came out of cloud I saw the end of a splash in the sea which I assume was him.

As explained in Brian Lane's story, at this time 19 Squadron was equipped with the Spitfire Mk IB, and was frustrated with the aircraft's problematic cannon; George Unwin:

The cannons were a real headache. We wanted and needed them, no doubt about that, but we didn't need the stoppages! Eventually the Commander-in-Chief himself, Air Chief Marshal Dowding, flew over to Fowlmere to talk to us about it and he listened carefully to what we had to say. Soon afterwards we were able to swap our Mk IBs with ordinary machine-gun armed Mk IAs, which came largely from an OTU.

Again as previously explained, after an engagement on 30 August, Squadron Leader Douglas Bader persuaded Air Vice-Marshal Leigh-Mallory to let him lead a three squadron strong 'Wing' of 12 Group fighters. So it was that 19 Squadron found itself being the Spitfire squadron assigned to this experiment. The intention was that the Hurricane squadrons, 242 and 310, would operate out of Duxford, while the Spitfires, based a short distance away at Fowlmere but with their superior performance, would operate as top cover. Contrary to some claims, there was no time lost to forming up, Squadron Leader Bader just set course and everyone did their best to follow him, despite the differences in individual aircraft performance. On 7 September, when the Germans began pounding London for the first time, Squadron Leader Bader led his formation into action for the first time. Although at a tactical disadvantage due to having been caught on the climb, battle was joined. Among the successful RAF pilots was Flight Sergeant Unwin.

Having initially attacked an Me 110, 'Grumpy' found himself alone at 4,000 feet. Climbing to 25,000, he saw a 'Hurricane squadron going somewhere in a hurry' and followed them. Suddenly three separate enemy formations comprising thirty bombers each, with their inevitable fighter escort, appeared. As the Hurricanes attacked the bombers, George found himself surrounded by Me 109s; fighting a running battle between Ramsgate and west London, he remembered:

> The usual fight ensued during which I definitely hit at least five of them but only two were shot down, both in flames. I then climbed for a breather and shadowed the third enemy formation when I saw yet a fourth arriving. By this time two of the other three formations had turned north and the other went straight on in a westerly direction. The leading formation turned east and I was at 25,000 feet and above them. As there did not seem to be any of their escorts left, I dived on the rear vic and gave them the rest of my ammunition, about 50 rounds in each gun, and from 450,

closing to 50 yards range. The bomber at which I fired wobbled a bit but otherwise carried on. Without ammunition, I then returned to Fowlmere.

Without crash locations, it is difficult to ascertain which Me 109s were destroyed by Flight Sergeant Unwin, although two of the three machines lost over England that afternoon by JG51 appear most likely. By the end of the day, 1,800 Londoners were dead or seriously injured. For Air Vice-Marshal Park this change in targets from his airfields to the capital was a miracle:

It was burning all down the river. It was a horrid sight. But I looked down and said 'Thank God for that', because I knew that the Nazis had switched their attack from our fighter stations thinking that they were knocked out. They weren't, but they were pretty groggy.

The attacks on London continued relentlessly, day and night. On 11 September, the 'Big Wing' was back in action, as George recalled for me nearly fifty years later:

I attacked a Dornier over London but was stupid enough to be shot down by the gunner they carried in a dustbin below the fuselage. I landed in a field near Brentwood in Essex and was taken to RAF North Weald by the army. With the aid of a fitter plus spares, 'QV-H' was repaired and I flew it back to Duxford two days later. One bullet had penetrated the armoured windscreen, however, so as this could not be repaired on station P9546 was then flown away to a Maintenance Unit. This Spitfire was one of those replacements for the Mk IBs that we received from the OTUs.

His forced-landing was much commended in the 19 Squadron ORB: 'Flight Sergeant Unwin made a wizard forced-landing with undercarriage down!!!!'

On 15 September, Flight Sergeant Unwin enjoyed considerable success. Some of 19 Squadron's Spitfires managed to engage the 109s, as had been planned; at 1210, over Westerham, Kent, George engaged 3/JG 53's Staffelkapitän, Oberleutnant Haase, in a dogfight:

I was Red Three with Flight Lieutenant Lawson. We sighted the enemy aircraft that were flying in vics of three. The escorts dived singly onto us and I engaged and Me 109 with a yellow nose. I gave one burst of six seconds and it burst into flames. The pilot baled out and the enemy aircraft crashed between Redhill and Westerham.

Haase was killed as his parachute failed to open.

During the next sortie that day, 'Grumpy' was Lane's Red 3 and reported sighting 'thousands of 109s'. When the Wing was attacked, at close range 'Grumpy' fired a three-second burst at a 109, which half-rolled and dived steeply into the clouds. Although the Spitfire pilot pursued his prey, he lost the 109 at 6,000 feet when his windscreen froze up. Climbing back up to 25,000, a rotte of 109s appeared above him, flying south. Flight Sergeant Unwin gave chase and caught both over Lydd. The first burst into flames and went down vertically, the second crashed into the sea. It is likely that these two 109s were from I/JG 77: Oberleutnant Kunze, of the Geschwaderstabschwarm, who was killed when his aircraft crashed at Lympne, as was Unteroffizier Meixner who crashed into the sea off Dungeness at about 1455. This brought Flight Sergeant Unwin's total of Me 109s definitely destroyed this day to three.

17 September saw the awards two gallantry decorations awarded to the Duxford squadrons: 310's Flight Lieutenant Jeffries received the DFC, and 19's Flight Sergeant George Unwin the DFM, his squadron's ORB commenting: 'Good show! Ten certain Huns to his credit.'

The majority of George Unwin's claims can be verified today and there can be no doubt that this award was much deserved. 'Grumpy' was undoubtedly among the most experienced Spitfire pilots in the RAF at this time.

On 18 September, George destroyed an Me 110, and on 27 September another 109.

The latter combat was a protracted dogfight lasting some ten minutes, and which took the Spitfire pilot dangerously near the French coast. Eventually George fired a 30° deflection shot. The 109 stalled and span into the sea.

Although British official sources consider that the Battle of Britain concluded on 31 October, the fact is that there are other dates apparently more appropriate. September 15, which was a decisive day as any and now celebrated annually as 'Battle of Britain Day', or 30 September, on which day the Germans conceded that they were unable to further sustain such heavy losses to its bomber force, are just two dates that spring readily to mind. Whatever, despite 31 October being chosen by the authorities, the fighter forces continued to clash over the south coast until early 1941.

On 5 November 1940, Flight Sergeant Unwin destroyed another Me 109, shared a 110 on 15 November, and a 109 on 28 November. By this time he was in Fighter Command's official list of successful pilots, and on 6 December a Bar to his DFM was gazetted. Later that month he was rested and left 19 Squadron to attend an instructor's course at Cranwell. All of this is remarkable considering that George joined the RAF as an airman, and during the Battle of Britain was twenty-seven-years old, much older than fighter pilot's average age. George gives his views at the end of the Battle of Britain:

> At the time I felt as though nothing out of the ordinary was happening. I had been trained for the job and fortunately already had a lot of flying experience. I was always most disappointed if the Squadron got into a scrap when I was off duty, and this applied to all of the pilots I knew. It was only after the event that I began to realise how serious defeat would have been, but we had never considered the prospect of defeat, it just wasn't possible in our eyes. That was simply our outlook at the time. As we lost pilots and aircraft, replacements were always forthcoming. Of course our new pilots were inexperienced, but so were the German replacements. It was clear at the end of 1940 that these pilots had not the stomach for a scrap with a Spitfire!

After such a successful time in 1940, and considering his age, many would consider that they had done enough. Indeed, there were a small number of pilots who disappeared into Training Command after their first operational tours, never to reappear on the front line scene. For both George Unwin and his 19 Squadron friend Harry Steere, however, such a prospect was intolerable. The pair made real fuss to get back on 'ops'. The slightly younger Steere achieved this in 1943, going to fly Mosquito Pathfinders, and George finally achieved his goal in April 1944, by threatening to transfer to Bomber Command! George then went to fly Mosquitoes too, but on night intruder operations with 613 Squadron. By then, however, Flight Lieutenant Harry Steere DFC DFM was dead, having been shot down over Rennes just three days after D-Day.

By VE Day, 'Grumpy' was Flight Lieutenant and there followed a series of instructing and staff appointments until his promotion to Squadron Leader in 1947, at which time he was posted overseas. Commanding 84 Squadron and flying Bristol Brigands, he flew operations during the Malayan Emergency, for service during which he received the DSO.

George Unwin's Battle of Britain combat claims largely tally with German actual losses, and yet so little has been written about him. George never sought or wanted recognition, or ever wrote a memoir. Nonetheless, this man was a true professional and an aggressive, gifted fighter pilot, make no mistake.

Sadly, shortly after our last meeting, 'Grumpy' died in June 2006, aged ninety-three. Having been friends for twenty years, it was an honour to speak at his funeral when I was able to justifiably describe George Unwin as the 'Finest of the Few'.

12

SERGEANT D.G.S.R. COX: 19 SQUADRON, SPITFIRE PILOT

David George Samuel Cox, from Cambridge, had attended Bournemouth School and joined the RAFVR while working as a solicitor's clerk. Called up on 1 September 1939, he completed his flying training and was posted to 19 Squadron, at Duxford, on 23 May 1940. The twenty-year old was this proud regular unit's first VR pilot, and it was the Squadron's task to make him combat ready:

> When I joined 19 Squadron, I was engaged on Operation DYNAMO, the air operation in support of the Dunkirk evacuation and was operating out of Hornchurch. Because I had not received any Spitfire training, however, I was unable to participate, so was given the job of ferrying replacement Spitfires to Hornchurch or testing those that had been repaired.

19 Squadron, the first unit to receive the Spitfire back in August 1938, was based at Fowlmere Farm, the satellite of Duxford Sector Station, near Cambridge, in 12 Group. Early on in the Battle of Britain, Duxford's squadrons often flew daily to aerodromes on the

east coast, such as Coltishall, from where they provided standing patrols over Channel bound convoys. The fighting, however, was taking place further south, particularly over the Dover area, which became appropriately known as 'Hellfire Corner'. Anxious for 12 Group to get some action, on 13 August, the Group Commander, Air Vice-Marshal Leigh-Mallory, arranged for 'B' Flight of 19 Squadron to fly across to Eastchurch, near Sheerness, from where the Spitfires were to participate in an attack on German E-boats near Calais. In an example of the Luftwaffe's poor intelligence, Eastchurch (which was not an important sector or indeed even a fighter station) was heavily bombed. David remembers:

> I was awakened by the bombing at about 0730. I rushed out of my room, which was in a wooden hut, into a corridor where I met Flight Sergeant Tofts, a pre-war professional airman who was in charge of the servicing of 'B' Flight's aircraft. He grabbed me by the arm and we ran into the only brick shelter available, a urinal, and Tofts pushed me to the floor, saying 'This is no time to be squeamish, lad!' Apparently 250 bombs were dropped and the airfield was strafed. There were 30 odd casualties although fortunately none from 19 Squadron.

The proposed attack against the E-boats was cancelled, and 'B' Flight returned to Fowlmere. On 15 August, Sergeant Cox was among the 19 Squadron pilots scrambled:

> The Squadron was scrambled to intercept a raid on Martlesham Heath airfield. The attack was carried out by some 25 Me 110s of Erprobungsgruppe 210, led by their brilliant commander

Hauptmann Rubensdörffer. The enemy were completely undetected until only a few minutes from the target. Only three Hurricanes of 17 Squadron managed to get airborne before the 110s arrived over the airfield. Our chances of intercepting the raid were nil, taking into consideration that Fowlmere to Martlesham was 60 air miles. Taking an optimistic speed for our Spitfires as 300 mph, it would take 12 minutes from take off to reach Martlesham. I doubt that at 2,000 feet our troublesome cannon-armed Mk IBs were capable of that speed anyway, as maximum speed was not reached until 19,000 feet. I would suggest that 280 mph was the maximum speed achievable at the given height, but even at 300 mph 19 Squadron could not achieve the impossible.

It was the start of increasing problems between 11 and 12 Groups. The System provided for 11 Group to make the forward interception, and while the fighters were up it was the responsibility of 12 Group to cover the 11 Group airfields. 12 Group, however, felt that 11 Group was attempting to hog the battle by only calling for assistance when absolutely necessary, by which time, as on 15 August, when it was too late given time, speed and distance. On 26 August, 19 Squadron was called upon to patrol the 11 Group Sector Station at Debden, as David remembered:

We were instructed by 11 Group to patrol at 10,000 feet, but the actual raid came in at 1,000 feet. As 19 Squadron was nine thousand feet higher and above a complete 10/10ths covering of cloud, we saw nothing of what went on. Apparently the Observer Corps had reported a raid incoming at 1,000 feet, but the 11 Group controllers assumed this to be a mistake and vectored us to

Angels 10 (height measured in thousands of feet). The subsequent intelligence report stated that 'the Spitfires from Fowlmere were slow in getting off the ground', which was absolutely not the case.

On 31 August, Fighter Command suffered its highest losses during the Battle of Britain:

We of 19 Squadron were caught on the hop! Most of us were still in bed as the Squadron was in a state of 'Stood Down'. We got a panic message to scramble at once. I put on my flying boots and jacket over my pyjamas. We took off at about 0800 and climbed south to Angels 17. It was jolly cold up there as the flying jacket only came down to my waist!

We soon sighted the enemy, about 30 Dorniers escorted by a large number of Me 110s above and behind. I was No 3 in Blue Section, which was led by Flying Officer James Coward. We were above and behind the bombers but below the 110s. We were put into echelon starboard and dived onto a section of bombers. Before I could open fire I was attacked by the 110s, so I took evasive action, a very, very sharp left-hand climbing turn, after which I found myself alone and no longer in contact with the Squadron.

I then climbed up to about 20,000 feet and flew southeast. Over Clacton I saw about 20–30 110s milling around in a left-hand circle, about 2,000 feet below me. I dived onto the circle and fired at one 110 that had got detached from the formation. My cannons operated perfectly as I was keeping a straight line without turning. The 110 turned sharply to port and then dived away steeply with his port engine belching black smoke. I was then attacked by four other 110s and so, being out of ammunition, got the hell out of it!

Apparently the 110 that I shot down belonged to II/ZG 76, the crew of which were both rescued from the sea and captured.

When I got back to Fowlmere I landed over the smoking remains of 19-year old Pilot Officer Aeberhardt's Spitfire. Having had some success in this engagement he crashed on landing due to being unaware of certain damage to his machine, flaps I think. After the war I visited his grave several times at Whittlesford churchyard. At first it was on its own with a large headstone and was well looked after. After about 20 years it became overgrown and obviously uncared for. I tidied it up myself and put some flowers on it. The last time I visited, Pilot Officer Aeberhardt's remains had been moved to lie amongst the other RAF graves and was, like them, carefully tended.

On 15 September, the Duxford-based 'Big Wing', led by Douglas Bader and including the Spitfires of 19 Squadron, now absorbed the Hurricanes of 302 (Polish) and the Spitfires of 611 Squadrons. On 'Battle of Britain Day', this Wing of sixty fighters arrived over the capital en masse. Sergeant Cox was among them:

> Now that was pretty inspiring, you must admit, all of us following Bader and arriving over the capital like that! I well remember the words of Bobby Oxspring, then a Flying Officer in an 11 Group Spitfire squadron, 66, exclaiming what a wonderful sight it was to see us appear. We must have given the German aircrews, who had been told that we were down to our last handful of fighters, one hell of a shock!

On 27 September, there were three major attacks mounted against London, and another raid headed for Filton in the West Country. David Cox:

I had jumped into the nearest Spitfire, X4237, 'QV–L', as mine would not start. This aircraft was nearly always flown by Sergeant Plzak, the six feet and six inches tall Czech who had dubbed me 'Little Boy'. To save time I buckled on his parachute which was already in the cockpit – more of that later!

19 Squadron took off just before noon and we were the Duxford Wing's top cover. It was in the area of Dover that a large number of Me 109s attacked us from above. After some hectic moments avoiding being shot down, I found myself more or less on my own between Ashford and Folkestone. Towards the latter I saw a Hurricane being set upon by four 109s, but before I could provide assistance, which was my intention having got within a few hundred yards of the scrap, the Hurricane went down in a vertical dive. This was a 242 Squadron aircraft flown by Pilot Officer Michael Homer DFC, who was killed when his machine crashed at Sittingbourne.

The four 109s then turned their attention to me. They knew their stuff as two got above me and two below. Naturally I had some hectic moments of turning this way and that as they came at me in attacks from all directions. I remember doing a lot of firing, but it was more in the hope of frightening them or raising my morale than in any real hope of shooting anything down!

All of a sudden there was a loud bang in the cockpit and for a second or two I was dazed. When I resumed normal there was a lot of smoke and my Spitfire was in a steep dive. I grabbed the control column and went up in a steep climb. As I lost flying speed I opened the hood, turned the aircraft over, undid my straps and fell out, quickly pulling the rip chord of my parachute. When the canopy opened it gave me a severe jolt, and several days later a lot of bruises showed on my chest and shoulders. Remember that the parachute harness was set for a man of six-and-a-half feet tall, I was lucky not to fall out of it!

As I floated down a 109 came and had a look at me and then flew off. It was then that I felt a lot of pain in my right leg and saw lots of holes in my flying boots out of which blood was oozing. Ground observers say that I took about 15 minutes to come down as I was so high up – I know that it was jolly cold up there when I came out of the aeroplane. I landed in the corner of a ploughed field near a farm at Walsford, near Ashford. Two farm hands carried me into the farmhouse. By this time I was feeling rather rough and must have looked it as the farmer handed me a bottle of whisky, from which I took a large swig. I was later taken to hospital at Walsford where a surgeon from Folkestone Hospital extracted several large pieces of cannon shell from just below my kneecap down into my ankle. I was in hospital about six weeks and off flying until December 1940. By coincidence, the next time I was shot down was on Friday 27th June, 1941, again in a Spitfire coded 'QV–L'!

Pilot Officer Eric Burgoyne, who was killed in this action, is buried in the churchyard at Burghfield. I have visited his grave, which is in a quiet spot underneath a large oak tree. He joined 19 Squadron on the same day as Pilot Officer Sutherland, Sergeant Roden and myself. Of the four I am the only survivor.

So ended David Cox's Battle of Britain, during which he destroyed an Me 110 and an Me 109. So, all these years later, what does he think of the controversial 'Big Wing', which, we now know, literally flew in the face of the Commander-in-Chief's System:

> When the Wing went into action the Spitfires kept the escorting fighters busy whilst the Hurricanes went for the bombers. This was right, I think, as the Spitfires were better suited from a performance perspective to tackle the 109s, whereas the Hurricanes would have been disadvantaged. Five squadrons were too many, I think. Three was OK, but why not three Spitfire squadrons, all therefore with identical performance? Spitfire squadrons would have made the allotted patrol lines faster and with the advantage of more height. That having been said, I do think that 11 Group could often have called for us earlier on. There is no doubt that many 11 Group personnel blamed the Wing's late arrival for their airfields being bombed. This caused bad feeling even between pilots. Even as late as the 1960s I got punched on the nose at a pub in Grimsby by a former 41 Squadron pilot when he discovered that I had flown with the Big Wing!

On 21 April, 1945, David Cox was sent to Burma and given command of a Spitfire Wing. In five years this NCO VR pilot had risen to Wing Commander, had become a fighter 'ace' (having also served with distinction in North Africa) and received a DFC and Bar. Having also been decorated by the French with a Croix de Guerre, Wing Commander Cox left the RAF in 1946, and went home to his wife, Pat. Like the other veterans featured in this book, David never forgot his combat flying, which must surely represent the most exciting, but uncertain, period of their lives. On 15 September 1980, the MOD permitted David Cox to fly over London as second pilot in a front line RAF Lightning jet interceptor. Forty years previously David had been over London in a Spitfire, in very different circumstances! In 1988, he participated in a 'Jim'll Fix It' television programme, during which David flew in the Grace Spitfire, ML407. It came as no surprise to hear that David had taken the controls, but how could we, we mortals who have never flown to battle in a Spitfire, imagine the myriad of nostalgic emotions that this remarkable man felt at that awesome moment?

David Cox was among my earliest correspondents, and this chapter was written from the bulging file of letters arising and from notes made during our various meetings at his comfortable Berkshire home. Sadly he died recently.

13

PILOT OFFICER K.A. LAWRENCE: 234/603 SQUADRONS, SPITFIRE PILOT

In addition to the British and free pilots from the occupied lands who fought in 1940, we must also remember those from the Commonwealth who came to help fight our 'bush fire'. For example, 4,000 New Zealanders served with the RAF during the Second World War; many perished, but Keith Ashley Lawrence numbers among the survivors.

Born on 25 November 1919, and educated at Invercargill, Keith applied to join the regular RAF via the Direct Entry Commonwealth Recruiting Scheme in 1938. In March 1939, therefore, he joined a contingent of 'Kiwis' sent to train with the RAF in England. Afterwards, in November, he was granted a Short Service Commission and posted to 234 Squadron. At that time, 234 was equipped with the Bristol Blenheim, but exchanged these for the much more exciting Spitfire in March 1940.

During the Battle of Britain, 234 Squadron served throughout with 10 Group, initially at St Eval, flying from where Pilot Officer Lawrence opened his account of enemy aircraft destroyed, then at Middle Wallop from 14 August onwards. As opposed to the situation between 11 and 12 Groups, there was an excellent spirit of co-operation between 11 and 10 Groups, and so it was that 11 Group frequently called upon 10 Group's squadrons to assist with interceptions over the capital and south-east. On 7 September, 234 Squadron was scrambled to assist in the defence of London, and on that day Keith was credited with having destroyed an Me 109 and damaged a Do 17. Two days later, however, 234 returned to St Eval, in Cornwall, but Keith was posted to 603 Squadron at Hornchurch. On 15 September, he destroyed an Me 109 and damaged two more. The young New Zealander was not to remain there long, however, as Keith relates:

On October 8th 1940, and at the instigation of the Prime Minister, No 421 Flight was formed at Gravesend. Known as the 'Jim Crow Flight', the unit had been formed largely from a detached flight of 66 Squadron, and was equipped with the new Spitfire Mk II, but included pilots from throughout Fighter Command who had fought in the Battle of Britain. Posted to the unit upon formation, I found that our purpose, flying singly or in pairs, was to report on the movement of enemy shipping in the Channel, or the build-up of Luftwaffe formations. Conjecture is that here was cover to permit ULTRA secrets to be used to best advantage but without giving the game away.

The proposed German invasion of England was called off on 12 October, and the Battle of Britain officially ended on 31 October. There was no respite however, and in fact, for the fighter forces of either side, which continued to engage over the South Coast until the weather really closed in during early 1941. Indeed, so far as November and December 1940 were concerned, they have rightly been called the *Forgotten Months* (a book by John Foreman, Air Research Publications, 1989).

By November 1940, we were stationed at RAF Hawkinge, on the high ground above the Straits of Dover. The Flight's first daily task was for a single Spitfire to fly a weather patrol along the Kentish coast between North Foreland and Dungeness to obtain met 'actuals' on the cloud conditions and formations. At the same time we would listen out for any operational instructions from control. The pilot detailed for the weather flight would take off between first light and sunrise.

On the morning of 27 November, I get airborne into a cloudy sky and fly uneventfully northeastwards to North Foreland and then turn 180 degrees at about 8,000 feet in the direction of Dungeness. There being nothing on the R/T to warn or distract, I cannot but be aware of the beauty, loneliness and apparent peacefulness which one experiences when flying between layers of cloud at that height, more so in the half light preceding sunrise. With not a sound in my headphones, but on constant lookout, I head towards Deal, still at 8,000 feet, and flying above some 5/10 stratocu and with 10/10 cumulous and stratocumulous overhead.

Suddenly, one corner of that scene turns from tranquillity to action, in a second! There, slightly on my port side, 500 feet below, through a gap in the cloud and streaking eastwards towards France, are three Me 109s in fairly close formation! At that speed not a second to lose, full throttle, stuff the nose down, switch on reflector sight and draw a bead. I start firing, three, maybe four seconds. An instant later I am falling earthwards in my stocking feet, slightly to my right I glimpse the rotating wing of my aircraft, falling as if a leaf. Come on now, get things in the right order! Parachute, 'D' ring on left-hand side, so reach across for it with right hand. Right hand won't move. Try assisting right hand with left hand... I am still falling (presumably by this time at terminal velocity, 120 mph) so must get a move on. I scrabble around with my left hand, trying to get at the left-sided release handle that will release my chute.

Success! The proverbial sigh of relief cut short as I realise that I am fast drifting in a westerly wind over the coast and out to a sea capped with white waves. Minutes later I am plunged into the cold, cold sea of late November, about a mile from land. With my right arm useless I must, left-handed, find the tube with which to inflate my life jacket, unbuckle my parachute harness and somehow keep my head above water. Within minutes I am coughing, spluttering, choking, and swallowing much seawater. The parachute shroud lines are everywhere, like a web. The Mae West does not inflate, its bladder evidently split by the ejection force on my Sutton harness, which supposedly holds the pilot firmly in the cockpit. With just the use of one arm and one leg, it seems that I am losing, engulfed in the cold wateriness that I cannot rise above.

Suddenly what seems like a high dark wall is looming over me, from which extends an arm of great strength to haul me bodily onto a boat manned by sailors of the Royal Navy.

Thereafter Keith, a lucky man indeed, was treated at Ramsgate Hospital with a fractured right leg, lacerated left leg and dislocated right shoulder. A week later he was transferred ninety miles west, 'most painfully and by an ambulance with solid tyres', to RAF Hospital Halton. It would be a year before Keith was considered fully recovered and fit enough to resume operational flying duties; he continues:

This simple recounting of an experience which was not unique, and befell many a pilot or other aircrew during wartime, tells but part of the story behind the announcement in the newspapers or on the radio, 'One of our aircraft was lost today', its background and consequences, one or two of which I now add as a footnote.

On the morning of this episode, my arrival at the airfield dispersal hut, being slightly less than punctual (as is the wont of some!), I just grabbed the first life jacket to hand. At that time, not all Mae Wests had been modified by the addition of a fluorescein dye packet. Fortunately the example that I picked up had been. My RN rescuers later told me that they first steered to my still inflated parachute, blowing across the surface, but on reaching it found no body. Only then, some distance away, did they sight my life-saving patch of bright fluorescent green seawater.

Also, many years later, when this escapade had become just another event in my distant past, I became aware of a group of aviation archaeologists who were trying to locate the remains of my Spitfire, which had apparently crashed near Finglesham, two miles north-west of Deal. By talking to the village's older inhabitants myself, I was able to ascertain that my crashing aircraft had caused no injury or loss of life.

Curiosity mounting, I decided to research for information about the sortie flown by the four German fighters that morning, 27 November 1940. The Dover Post of the Royal Observer Corps entry for 0700 hours that morning read 'Hostile heard'. Was my assailant one of a regular dawn patrol flown by a German schwarm over Kent? The answer to this question may well lie in the archives of the 'Y' Service, the intelligence unit that intercepted all enemy R/T transmissions. These transcripts, however, are closed to the public.

Be that as it may, available from German combat reports we do know that I was the victim of Oberleutnant Gustav 'Mickey' Sprick,

Staffelkapitän of 8/JG 26. He had been amongst the first German fighter pilots with 20 aerial victories and received his Knight's Cross accordingly on October 1st, 1940. On June 28th, 1941, however, the wing of his Me 109F collapsed during a dogfight over France, and he was killed in the resulting crash. Sprick's final tally was 31 victories.

After recovery and a Spitfire refresher course, I again made close acquaintance with JG 26 when I was posted to Malta. Based in Sicily, German bombers attacked Malta several times a day, their fighter escort often being provided by 7/JG 26.

What would have made the perfect postscript to this adventure for me would have been discovery of my RN rescuers and their ship. So this has so far not proved possible, but I give thanks, as must many other of my fellow pilots of those days.

After serving on Malta, Keith Lawrence was awarded the DFC, and he later flew dive-bombing sorties against German V2 rocket launching sites on the Dutch coast. After the war, he returned to his native New Zealand, serving as an air traffic controller in the Territorial Air Force. Later, he returned to England and a new life in Sussex, but now enjoys a peaceful retirement with his wife, Kay, in the West Country.

14

PILOT OFFICER R.L. JONES: 64/19 SQUADRONS, SPITFIRE PILOT

Richard Jones was a VR pilot who had learned to fly at Woodley, near Reading. There he flew Harts, Hind and Audax biplanes before progressing to the Magister monoplane. Mobilized on 1 September 1939, Richard's advanced service flying training was undertaken on Harvards at RAF Ternhill, in Shropshire. He was then taught how to fly Spitfires at 5 OTU, Aston Down (near Stroud in Gloucestershire). In July 1940, Pilot Officer Jones was posted to fly Spitfires with 64 Squadron:

Upon arrival at Kenley, I remember being met by the CO, an absolutely charming man and a real gentleman in every sense of the word, Squadron Leader Don MacDonell. He immediately made us new pilots feel at home, he called us his 'chicks'. We would find our CO a quiet but determined leader and an excellent fighter pilot. He looked after the best interests of all who served under him and he had the respect of all.

To give us battle experience as quickly as possible whenever the time allowed, we were paired off with a senior battle-experienced pilot to practise dog-fighting and yet more dog-fighting to give us both experience and confidence in the Spitfire and combat conditions. We were lucky to have that extra curricular training, which would have been impossible had we been posed to 64 later on that summer and for obvious reasons.

The operational focal point of every squadron was dispersal, which was a hut containing 12 beds, and an Orderly Clerk with a telephone. I well recall the three states of Readiness. The first was 'Readiness', which meant all pilots kitted up and ready to go. The next was at '15 minutes', which meant that you had to be in the Mess and available to be ready for flight in 15 minutes. Finally, '30 minutes', which meant that you could relax a bit, play billiards or go to the local cinema. From that state you could be called to '15 minutes' and so on.

If you were on Readiness, then that day you would rise very early, at around 4 a.m., so that you were at the aerodrome and ready before dawn in the event of an emergency. Immediately, you would be served a remarkable breakfast and the attention that we received from staff was amazing. After breakfast we used to get into what we called the 'Cattle Truck' to be driven over to Dispersal. We would then get kitted up, excepting our helmets and parachutes, which were placed on or in the aircraft, also at the ready, and waited in the Crew Room for something to happen. If you were not down on the board to fly, then it was a long day, waiting around. Most pilots spent their waiting time playing cards, chess, reading or sleeping. Suddenly the tranquillity would be shattered by the telephone's bell, Immediately everyone was tense, in anticipating of orders to scramble. Certainly the telephone stirred our senses quicker than anything else that I have ever experienced.

If it was a scramble, we ran to and got into our Spitfires, engines started and away. We would be given immediate instructions, such as 'Scramble Angels 10 over Dungeness'. We knew that because our radar based system of early warning, wherever we were sent there was always a good chance of meeting the enemy. If we did meet the Germans then of course we would engage them to the best of our ability.

When we came back, anybody who had been successful, perhaps in shooting down an enemy aircraft, might do such a thing as a 'victory roll', but those were not encouraged because it was not always known whether one's own aircraft was in fact damaged. Immediately upon landing the IO would take full details from each pilots of what had happened, whilst the groundcrew prepared the aircraft for immediate take-off. We then started the waiting process all over again, until such time as we were either scrambled again or relieved of Readiness by another squadron. We would then drop back to 15 minutes, then 30 minutes, and so the cycle went on. In fairness despite the actual state of Readiness, we were always pretty much ready for most eventualities.

One incident of many that I can still recall was when we of 64 Squadron were visited by the Air Minister, Sir Archibald Sinclair. We were all lined up to meet him, standing in front of our Spitfires. He congratulated us on the work that we were doing and in his opening words thanked us as Hurricane pilots of 12 Group! Clearly the Minister knew not the difference between a Spitfire or Hurricane, much less the disposition of Fighter Command's Groups. We were not impressed.

On 20 September, Pilot Officer Jones was posted from 64 to 19 Squadron at Fowlmere. By that time, as we have read before, 19 Squadron was operating as a top cover Spitfire squadron in Douglas Bader's so-called 'Big Wing'. Richard therefore enjoys an enviable perspective on the tactical argument of the day, having flown Spitfires during the Battle of Britain in both 11 and 12 Groups.

On 28 October, a single Gruppe of Ju 88s headed for London, protected by three Jagdgeschwadern of Me 109s. Soon 19 Squadron was up, Pilot Officer Jones flying Spitfire P7432:

When patrolling over the Tenterden area at 29,000 feet, the Controller informed us that as there were apparently no enemy aircraft in the vicinity we could 'pancake'. I was 'Arse-end Charlie' and relaxed slightly as we descended to 20,000 feet. Suddenly about four feet of my starboard wing just peeled off. My initial thought that it was a poor show on a new aircraft. Then a loud bang followed and a hole appeared above the undercarriage. I was obviously the target of an enemy fighter positioned up sun. Immediately I took evasive action but simultaneously my engine cut out, so suddenly I was in a high speed stall and spin. As my radio was U/S I was unable to inform the Squadron, the other pilots of which returned to base blissfully unaware that I had been shot down.

As the aircraft's controls were not responding I did not recover from the spin until at 10,000 feet, and at that time I realised that the hood was jammed shut. Subsequently I crash-landed with a dead engine in one of only two suitable fields in a heavily wooded area just outside Hawkhurst. Unfortunately I did so amongst a flock of sheep and unfortunately several were killed. I was rescued by the Army and taken first to the Hawkhurst doctor who treated a flesh wound to my leg, then to their Mess prior to returning safely to Fowlmere.

My Spitfire had a broken propeller and radiator, a few holes and some missing parts but was otherwise relatively undamaged. For some reason the incident was not recorded in the 19 Squadron ORB, but in my logbook I wrote 'Shot down and crash-landed at Hawkhurst, Kent. Killed three sheep. What a bloody mess!!!', which it was.

On 15 November, Richard was returned to 64 Squadron, with which he remained until April 1941, when seconded to the Ministry of Aircraft Production and 'lent' to the De Havilland company as a test pilot. Consequently Richard test flew Spitfires and Hurricanes that had been repaired at the factory, a job which he retained until leaving the RAF (as a Flight Lieutenant) in 1946.

Now long retired from a post war career in the motor industry and a long spell as a part-time court usher, although in his 90s, Richard continues to enjoy life and retirement in Oxfordshire.

15

SERGEANTS D.H. NICHOLS & P.H. FOX: 56 SQUADRON, HURRICANE PILOTS

Writing about yet more VR sergeants, Denis 'Nick' Nichols and Peter Fox, emphasizes just how many such pilots fought in the Battle of Britain. Without them it would have been impossible to make good losses, so clearly the far-sightedness that led to the creation of this part-time force paid off.

'Nick' joined the VR in 1938, and completed his elementary flying training at Sywell in Northamptonshire. On 1 September 1939, he too was called to full time service along with many other reservists, including Peter Fox and Ken Wilkinson. The threesome would go through their service flying training together. Having completed this at Montrose, on 1 September 1940, Nichols and Fox moved on to 6 OTU at Sutton Bridge, where they learned to fly the Hurricane, while Wilkinson (more of whom later) went to 7 OTU and Spitfires at Hawarden. Just a fortnight later, on 15 September, Sergeants Nichols and Fox, both of whom were nineteen, reported to 56 Squadron at RAF Boscombe Down in Dorset. The day afterwards, these two young fighter pilots were introduced to the grim realities of service on an operational fighter squadron when they performed duty as pall bearers at the funeral of a fellow NCO pilot who had been accidentally killed during dogfight practice.

No. 56 Squadron was a regular fighter squadron with a proud tradition dating back to the Great War. Like 151, the other North Weald Hurricane squadron of the time, 56 had not only fought in France but was also heavily engaged throughout the early part of the Battle of Britain. Casualties had been high, however, and some fine airmen lost, men like Flight Lieutenant Percy 'Mouse' Weaver DFC, who failed to return from an engagement on 31 August. The following day, 56 was rested and sent to recuperate at Boscombe Down in 10 Group. Replacement pilots were received there and these 'sprogs' had the opportunity to receive further training by the Squadron. As Sergeants Nichols and Fox would soon discover, the prospect of combat over the West Country remained a distinct possibility.

On 30 September, the Germans made their last massed formation raid in daylight. The target was the Westland Aircraft Factory at Yeovil in Somerset. Unfortunately, however, cloud obscured the target, leading to an unfortunate navigational error that led to bombs cascading not on the intended target but on the nearby town of Sherborne in Dorset. Among the RAF fighters scrambled in response was 56 Squadron, and Sergeant Fox would soon catch his first glimpse of the enemy:

> I just couldn't believe it. There were about 40 He 111s of KG55, together with escorting Me 110s, approaching Lyme Bay, inbound. I selected one of the rearmost bombers, aimed firstly at one engine, pressed the gun button and sprayed across to the other. The enemy aircraft slowed significantly and peeled off to port. I followed, still

firing, when suddenly there was an explosion and I noted that there was little left of my instrument panel! Fortunately my hood was already half open, which prevented any chance of it jamming shut in the event of the cockpit being so damaged. I broke to starboard, upwards and away, with all controls apparently functioning correctly. I got over land at 3,000 feet and was wondering whether I could make the coastal airfield at Warmwell (near Weymouth), when I saw flames coming up between my legs. I don't think that I even thought about my next action, which was to instinctively roll the kite upside down and release my harness. I then saw my feet still above me, and the Hurricane above my feet, presumably stalled. Where was the rip chord? I told myself to calm down, and pulled the 'D' ring straightaway. I had never before pulled a rip chord, never seen one pulled, never seen a parachute packed, and never had any instruction! The 'D' ring was flung into the air, followed by some wire. Obviously I had broken it! I then felt the tug of the pilot chute followed almost immediately by the wrench of the main parachute. I was safe! The next second I was aware of an 'enemy', which I assumed was going to shoot me. It was, however, my flaming Hurricane, which literally missed me by inches! The kite slowly screwed round, going into a steeper and steeper dive until almost vertical, aimed directly at the cross-hedges of four fields to the north-east of a wood towards which I was drifting. The aircraft hit the cross-hedges spot on, a short pause then a huge explosion followed by another pause before flames shot up to a great height. I'm glad that I wasn't in it!

I was safe again but didn't feel it as the sea looked rather close and I didn't want to end up swimming. I then recalled a film about a German parachutist, which had shown how if you pulled the parachute lines on one side or the other, the direction was slipped off accordingly. I tried, but which side I don't know as I could not see which way I was drifting. I certainly could not think aerodynamically at that moment! Leave well alone, I thought! I was safe again, then, blood! Trickling down my right leg. I tried to lift my right leg to see, but couldn't. I'd met aircrew who had lost limbs but could still feel extremities that were no longer there. My leg must have been shot off and would crumble beneath me upon landing! I was getting close to the ground and worried about my 'shot off' leg when I remembered the story of a pilot being shot in the foot by the Home Guard. 'BRITISH!' I shouted at the top of my voice. I pulled hard as my parachute clipped a tree on the edge of a wood. Upon landing I just fell over gently, when the wind pulled the chute sideways, and I shouted 'BRITISH!' again. As no one came I started to roll up my parachute when a farm labourer climbed over a nearby fence and requested confirmation that I was okay.

My 'shot off' leg was not, in fact, 'shot off'. It was just a tiny wound on my knee where a small piece of shrapnel had entered, and another the same size also half an inch away where it had come out. A lady with a horse then came along and I draped my parachute over the animal. Off we went on foot until a van took me to Lyme Regis Police Station. I was then entertained in the local pub whilst I awaited transport back to Warmwell. Someone from Air Sea Rescue arrived and I told him that I was pretty sure that 'my' Heinkel had gone into the drink.

Peter had probably been bounced by either an Me 109 or a 110. A week later, the Germans tried to hit Westlands again, this time with twenty Ju 88s of II/KG 51. Once more 56 Squadron joined the fray, and this time it was Sergeant Nichols' turn to meet the enemy. At 1530 hours, 'Nick' and four other Hurricanes were scrambled from Warmwell (from which forward airfield 56 operated on a daily basis):

We took off in formation with me on the left of the leader, Flight Lieutenant Brooker, and I was 'Pip-squeak' man, my radio being blocked every 15 seconds. I can't remember hearing any R/T transmissions so perhaps the wireless was on the blink. I did not even hear the 'Tally ho!'. Flying in tight formation the first I saw was tracer coming from our leader's guns. Quick glimpse and I saw a Ju 88 and fired, still in formation, but had to break away to avoid collision with the Flight Lieutenant. I then lost the Squadron and pulled up, searching for the enemy. No sign of the bombers but 110s in a defensive spiral above. I pulled the 'tit' for maximum power and went to intercept.

A Spitfire was attacking the top of the spiral so I went head-on for the bottom. I fired but, perhaps not surprisingly in view of their heavy forward firing armament that I must have overlooked, was hit. Flames poured from the nose of my aircraft and the windscreen was black with oil, so I broke away as I could not see out. I turned the aircraft on its back to bale out at 25,000 feet. First time a slow roll but I remained seated. Second time I tumbled out, spinning. I told myself not to panic and gave the rip chord a steady pull. When the parachute deployed, the lanyards on one side were twisted. I tried to untangle them without success but relaxed, as at about 15,000 feet I appeared to be coming down reasonably slowly. I did not see the ground ultimately rush up at me and crumpled in a heap upon landing.

The Home Guard then appeared on the scene and told me to stick my hands up. They thought I was German but I just laughed at them between groans as I had actually broken my back. There was a Jerry parachutist stuck up a nearby tree, from the Ju 88, but the locals refused to get him down until they had seen to me.

Nick had landed near the village of Alton Pancras on the Dorset Downs. At about 1600 hours, Charlie Callaway, coincidentally another nineteen-year old, was ploughing in the 'Vernall' when he saw the Hurricane 'coming down hard and well on fire!' His younger brother Sam, seventeen, was rabbiting nearby and he too saw the doomed British fighter 'descending at a shallow angle but all ablaze and travelling sharpish like. It was so close that I could have reached out and touched it. There were several parachutes in the sky at the same time.' Nick's Hurricane, P3154, impacted at Austral Farm, some nine miles north of Dorchester.

Despite Nick's back injury, both he and Peter were lucky: both had met the enemy on their first operational patrol; both had been shot down but they had survived.

Later, Peter Fox also broke his back while serving with 56 Squadron, when he was 'flown into a haystack'. Recovered, he later went on to fly Spitfires with 234 Squadron, also out of Warmwell, until he was shot down by ground fire on 20 October 1941, while crossing over the French coast near Cherbourg on a 'Rhubarb'. Fortunately Peter made a safe forced-landing and spent the remainder of the war in captivity. Unfortunately this mishap was the last in a string of events that prevented him from being commissioned, so it was with the rank of Warrant Officer that Peter ultimately left the RAF after the war.

Nick also recovered from his broken back and went back to operational flying. Instead of single-engine fighters, however, he found himself patrolling nocturnal skies over North Africa and later the Mediterranean in a 255 Squadron Bristol Beaufighter. He was not to meet the enemy again, but was more fortunate than Peter given that Nick was commissioned in March 1942. After the war he became an airline pilot and so flew throughout his working life.

It was from talking to Nick that I first became particularly interested in the raids against Westlands on 30 September and 7 October 1940. At the time I was actively involved in aviation archaeology and interested in investigating the crash site of his Hurricane. When I first explained our intention to Nick, his first reaction was: 'I threw it away in 1940 and I don't want it back now!' In time, however, he became increasingly interested in the project, to the extent that he accepted our invitation to join the (former) Malvern Spitfire Team for the excavation in November 1993.

At Austral Farm we received a warm and kindly welcome from the Ralphs, and the villagers treated Nick like a king. He was both surprised and moved by this exhibition of respect and appreciation. We were not, however, the first enthusiasts to examine the site, at which comparatively little was left due to the nature of the crash. Many smashed components of the Hurricane were found, however, including a piece of armoured glass windscreen, through which Nick had last peered over fifty years before at the wrong end of an Me 110. Another Battle of Britain pilot, Squadron Leader Iain Hutchinson, who had flown Spitfires with 222 Squadron, and German veteran Hans 'Peter' Wulff joined us at the site. The latter was formerly a Luftwaffe Leutnant who had flown He 111s against the Russians, and Me 410s and FW 190s against the west until shot down and captured on Operation Bodenplatte, New Year's Day 1945. Peter had made his home in England after the war and was a true aviation enthusiast, having flown every year of his life, excepting 1946, since learning to glide with the Hitler Youth. It was tremendous that Peter was welcomed by the two British veterans, not as an enemy but as a fellow enthusiast and combat pilot who shared their common bond. Television cameras and reporters swarmed over the site, and with pilots and eyewitnesses present the events of 7 October 1940, were vividly brought back to life as all remembered that dramatic day.

It was not until November 1995, however, that we got around to returning Peter to his Wootten Fitzpaine crash site. The remains of his N2434 'US-H' was found exactly where Peter had described it, at the cross-hedges of four fields. Although smashed to pieces, many items were found, including eyelets from Peter's Sutton harness. At the site Peter and his wife Beryl, herself a wartime WAAF, were able to meet eyewitnesses who excitedly related their recollections, and rekindle acquaintance with the ever popular and gentlemanly Peter Wulff. Once more the excavation attracted much media interest, and was broadcast as a news item the length of Britain's south coast. For Peter there was a bonus: having been made an honorary member of the Malvern Spitfire Team, we had applied to the MOD for ownership of N2434 to be transferred from the Crown to Peter himself. So it was that we were also able to pass Peter the official documentation confirming this to be the case, making him the only one of the Few to own his Battle of Britain aircraft!

Sadly, our German friend Peter Wulff died in 1997, since when both Denis Nichols and Peter Fox have joined him in that great hangar in the sky.

16

SERGEANT K.A. WILKINSON: 616/19 SQUADRONS, SPITFIRE PILOT

Ken Wilkinson, who trained with Peter Fox and Denis Nichols, describes his personal route to the cockpit:

Sitting in a classroom at school there was a tendency to take no notice of what gems of knowledge were being handed out, because it was far more important to be able to draw a recognisable side view of a fighter aircraft! It was Cheltenham Grammar School and there was plenty of opportunity because Gloster Aircraft was only a few miles away at Brockworth where Gamecocks and Gauntlets were being tested. There was also the Gloster entrant to the Schneider Trophy, which, although it did not fly over Cheltenham, inspired us nonetheless and its outline was well known to us.

Then, when I was 17, my father asked if I would like to fly as a pilot in the RAF, to which there could only ever be one answer. Being a junior in an insurance office lost whatever minimal appeal it may previously have had. The application for a Short Service Commission went in when I was exactly 17¾ years of age and then my father said, 'If you want to fly for a living then you'd better find out more about it.' Five bobsworth with Alan Cobham's Flying Circus was not considered sufficient!

In April 1936, I went to Brockworth and was introduced to the test pilot 'Mr Summers' (now there's a name for you, he who first flew the Spitfire!) and put in the gunner's seat of a Hawker Hart Beeste, which was a variant produced for the South African Air Force. I was much too excited to worry about the seemingly inadequate clip that secured me to the seat, and don't think I really absorbed what was being told me about the parachute. I addressed Mr Summers as 'Sir' every time he spoke to me, clearly preparing myself for the deference to be paid to the officer set over me in the future.

The next half-hour was wonderful. Medium turns, steep turns, rolls, loops, dives etc and all looking backwards with no way of knowing what was coming next! Every pilot knows the feeling of being above the clouds for the first time – it's even better looking backwards! When I was later given formal air experience on a Tiger Moth, I recall being somewhat blasé about it all.

After landing I expressed my gratitude in as profuse a manner as I could manage to Mr Summers and to my father who had arranged it. Afterwards it was back to being a junior in an insurance office with even less interest than before, having now had the great experience of flight in a fighting machine. There were those who had gone to great lengths to ensure that I got the experience, but I felt that inner superiority over those earthbound creatures who had not shared my experience.

Later on I discovered that none of Gloster Aircraft's employees ever volunteered for passenger duties and the test pilots did not like flying with a sack on the back seat, so I was actually helping them by taking the flight.

I did not, in fact, get a commission at that time, but joined the VR and learnt to fly at Staverton. On September 1st 1939, I was called up, and completed my service flying training, with Denis Nichols and Peter Fox, between May and August 1940. Then it was off to 7 OTU, Hawarden and Spitfires, before joining 616 Squadron at Kirton.

616 Squadron was an auxiliary unit which had been heavily engaged during August 1940 while flying from Kenley (as described in the chapter concerning William Walker). Losses were extremely high, and when the Squadron was withdrawn on 3 September, only eight of its original pilots had survived. After a brief spell at Coltishall, 616 settled in at Kirton where it became categorized a 'C' unit. On 7 September, Air Chief Marshal Dowding and other officers of Air rank held the 'Going downhill conference', so called because of the recognition of the fact that there were not enough combat ready replacement pilots. The OTUs were working flat out, but were still not producing enough pilots, in spite of all the short cuts. The solution arrived at by Air Chief Marshal Dowding and Air Vice-Marshal Park, the Commander-in-Chief of 11 Group, was to categorize fighter squadrons 'A', 'B' or 'C' units. 'A' were those in the front line and maintained with a minimum strength of sixteen pilots, 'B' were those being rested but with a minimum of six combat ready pilots among the establishment of sixteen, and which could be called upon if necessary. 'C' were those unlikely to be called into battle given that they were rebuilding to strength following losses suffered in the combat zone. The minimum number of combat ready pilots in a 'C' unit was three, and it was down to these men to pass on their experience to the new boys.

When Sergeant Wilkinson joined 616 Squadron, it was therefore being used as an extension of the OTU process, providing further training for a host of new pilots between the end of the actual OTU courses and a further posting to a squadron in the combat zone (as combat ready pilots). So it was that in October 1940, Ken moved on again, this time to fly Spitfires with 19 Squadron at Fowlmere:

When I arrived at Duxford there was a Hurricane beating the place up at very low level. I asked the guard who the pilot was, and without hesitation he said 'Squadron Leader Bader'. Of course I already knew of the great man by reputation, so thought 'Well, this is going to be interesting!'

Squadron Leader Brian Lane DFC, who was very popular, commanded 19 Squadron, and as an NCO I got to know people like George Unwin and Harry Steere. They were professional, pre-war, airmen, and both were superb fighter pilots.

Really, and probably fortunately for me upon reflection, I joined the Squadron a bit late on to see much action during the Battle of Britain, which was now coming to a close. Consequently I shot nothing down, but by the same token I did not get shot down myself, so I call it a 'no score draw'!

Early in 1941, Ken became an instructor at a FGS, returning to operational flying in 1943, initially with 234 Squadron and subsequently with 165 Squadron. With these units Ken, who had by now been commissioned, flew the usual round of operational sorties. After that tour, Ken became an instructor, ending up at Honeybourne in Worcestershire. There he flew Hurricanes on fighter affiliation exercises with Wellingtons from the OTU based there. Being a Midlander himself, and now married with a baby on the way, the arrangement suited Ken perfectly.

After the war, Ken became a surveyor. Now retired, he lives with his daughter, Penny, in the West Midlands and enjoys his golf most weeks. He is also an enthusiastic member of both the Battle of Britain Fighter Association and the Spitfire Society, and thoroughly enjoys representing the Few at various air shows and other events. We have also been together several times to tell primary school children about the Battle of Britain, and Ken's relaxed and amusing manner always helps to get the point across in a way the children will remember and understand.

One thing I will always remember about Ken Wilkinson is an occasion during which we were filming with Central TV News. Ken and fellow former Spitfire pilot Ron Rayner DFC were looking over a Merlin engine recovered from a Spitfire's crash site when spontaneously Ken put his arm around Ron and said: 'As a fighter pilot, you were a cocky bugger, but as a Spitfire pilot you were cockier still!' Some things, it seems and despite advancing years, don't change!

17

PILOT OFFICER W. CUNNINGHAM: 19 SQUADRON, SPITFIRE PILOT

Wallace 'Jock' Cunningham, from Glasgow, was a VR pilot officer who joined 19 Squadron at Duxford in June 1940. His first success came on 16 August, when he destroyed an Me 110, followed by an He 111 on 7 September, and Me 109s on both the 9th and 15th. Three days he shared a Ju 88, and on 8 October received the DFC. After the Battle of Britain, on 15 November, 19 and 242 Squadrons were detailed to patrol a convoy off Harwich, when the former was vectored to intercept bandits approaching England from the north-west and at 25,000 feet. Two condensation trails were spotted at 35,000 feet, fifteen to twenty miles apart, so the squadron separated into flights and gave chase. Red Section, comprising Squadron Leader Lane with Pilot Officers Cunningham and Vokes, chased the leading German, climbing south to get between the enemy and the sun. After a twenty minute chase up the Thames Estuary, the bandits were identified as Me 110s. Simultaneously spotting the Spitfires, the 110s turned east and dived. Lane ordered Red Section into line astern and attacked. Subsequently the enemy machine crashed into the Thames Estuary near Southend. Unteroffizier Boschen was killed, but the pilot,

Leutnant Heinz Jakob, was captured. 'B' Flight's target was also sent plunging into the estuary, its crew posted missing. During the action, Cunningham's Spitfire had been damaged:

> I was tucked in behind Brian Lane and diving after the fleeting Me 110. Because of our high speed Brian was struggling to get his sights on the target was almost jostling him off to get a chance. Before we eventually destroyed the enemy aircraft, after letting the pilot bale out, I had my armoured glass windscreen shattered. Not, we worked out later, by the enemy, but by Brian's empty cartridge cases!

The Thames Estuary was the scene of 19 Squadron's next but final combat of 1940, on 28 November, when the Spitfires clashed with 109s of I/JG26 'Schlageter'. With the onset of winter weather, 19 Squadron was not to make another combat claim until 27 June 1941, during the Fighter Command Offensive over France. On that day another 19 Squadron stalwart and Flight Commander, Flight Lieutenant 'Farmer' Lawson DFC, destroyed an Me 109 over Lille, as did Sergeant David Cox who was himself shot up. On 21 July, Sergeant Charnock destroyed an Me 109, followed by another on 7 August. In July, Lawson had been promoted to Squadron Leader and took command of 19 Squadron. Cunningham was promoted to flight lieutenant and became commander of 'B' Flight. In 1994, Wallace Cunningham remembered those days, a year after the desperate battles over England in 1940:

> I recall the high level sweeps over France, escorting a few Stirling bombers, so mildly offensive that the Germans did not put up

any fighters for us to tangle with. I remember also a fair number of low level trips to attack shipping off the Dutch coast. These were extravagant on Blenheim losses. There was one daylight raid on Cologne, I recall it positively because I had an abscess on my backside and a stye in my eye – very warlike I felt!

During this period we had German night raids on London and Coventry. We were up on some of these but the blinding effect of the glowing Spitfire exhausts right before the pilot's eyes made it both unpleasant and futile. Altogether these raids were very depressing – we could see the explosions of bombs, the ignition of incendiaries, but could not see the bombers. The technique approved was to sit below the AA flashes and hope to see the enemy aircraft silhouetted against them.

Of course we routinely flew up and down coastal convoys in the North Sea. The graveyard of Dogger Bank showed up the dangerous task of these underpaid, little appreciated merchant seamen. Hopefully our presence frightened off the odd raid. We sat at low level east of the convoys, looking into the setting sun. Any sign of an attacker and we made a great show, chasing off the poacher. Sometimes when it was judged too dark for the bombers we would be instructed to 'pancake' – a mile or two west of the convoy and we would see AA flashes. The bomber would have watched us against the setting sun and noted our departure.

I recall one thick, misty day over the North Sea trying to find a convoy. I would be vectored onto the convoy's position but at a height of several thousand feet which was necessary for radio contact with base. When I descended through the murk to try and find the convoy, trying to guess where fog stopped and sea started, no contact was made. This occupied me for a time but I guess that the controller decided that if I had so much difficulty, having the benefit of his assistance, then the convoy was safe from attack!

The squadron moved to Matlaske, a satellite of Coltishall, about the beginning of August 1941. We were billeted at Itteringham Mill, a beautiful house situated over a mill stream filled with trout. To Farmer Lawson and I this had all the appearance of a rest cure. The ante-room had a large open fireplace with inglenooks. I had a large and comfortable room with my own batman. I even had my dog there. Then we were sent on that stupid trip to Rotterdam.

On 21 August 1941, 19 Squadron re-equipped with Long Range Spitfire Mk IIAs, which were received from 234 Squadron. These new aircraft extended the squadron's operational range, so on 26 August, 19 Squadron escorted Blenheims across the North Sea to attack a convoy off the Dutch coast. The operation to Rotterdam docks on 28 August, however, was to prove extremely costly. 19 Squadron ORB:

1800 hrs: Squadron took off from Matlaske together with 12 long range Spits of 152 Squadron before rendezvousing with 17 Blenheims from 21, 89 and 11 Squadrons. Course was set to cross the Dutch coast south of Oostveine, the bombers being in three boxes of five, six and six at 2,000' with 19 Squadron in sections of four on their port side and 152 on the starboard side at 2,000'. The Dutch coast was crossed at 1900 hrs and the formation then turned to port so that the bombers could cross the target area, the Rotterdam docks, in line abreast. Whilst the bombers went in to bomb their target, 19 Squadron kept to the west to pick up the bombers as they came out. Very heavy flak was encountered over

Holland between Rotterdam and the coast both from the ground and ships in the river south of Rotterdam, particularly from a ship which appeared to be an armed merchantman. Some of the flak had a low trajectory of about 100 feet and range of about a mile. Pilot Officer Marsh reported seeing flak coming from a church tower. The result of the bombing was not observed as the squadron was not over the target area, but one bomber was seen to go down in flames.

The Blenheims certainly had it rough; 110 Squadron ORB:

Low-level attack made from 20 feet, and each aircraft dropped two 500 lb and four dropped 24 incendiaries. Aircraft 'H', flown by Sergeant Jenkinson, scored a direct hit on a red painted ship of 8,000 tons just off dock 14 – flame and bright red smoke was observed. During these operations, Wing Commander Cree reported seeing a Blenheim crash into a warehouse on the north-west corner of Maashaven, which started a large fire. The same pilot also reported seeing a Spitfire going down in flames. Aircraft 'H' reported a further Blenheim seen to crash into the river from low-level shortly afterwards. Considerable AA fire encountered and aircraft 'K' hit several times although damage not serious.

The Spitfire down was Sergeant Savidge of 152 Squadron. While all of 110 Squadron's Blenheims returned safely, 21 Squadron was not so lucky (ORB): 'Four of our aircraft did not return.' 19 Squadron ORB reported:

Whilst over Holland, Pilot Officers Marsh, Stuart and Strihavka shot up a ship in the river south of Rotterdam. Sergeant Charnock and Pilot Officer Edmunds shot up a machine-gun post each and Sergeant Sokol a factory. When the bombers came out from the target area they were escorted home. Pilot Officer Marsh landed 25 minutes after the rest of the squadron to report Squadron Leader Lawson DFC missing. Both pilots had apparently become separated from the rest of the squadron and were coming home on the starboard side of the bombers. When 15 miles off the Dutch coast, Pilot Officer Marsh saw his leader on the tail of an aircraft which he thought was a Spitfire. Squadron Leader Lawson did not appear to go into action and had no aircraft on his tail. Likewise there, was no flak, but Squadron Leader Lawson broke away and Pilot Officer Marsh did not see his leader again, so joined up with 152 Squadron and returned to base.

Squadron Leader Lawson was missing over the North Sea in Spitfire P7995. 6/JG53's Me 109s had been scrambled, and Feldwebels Krantz and Gothe each subsequently claimed Spitfires destroyed. One is believed to have been Lawson, the other a 41 Squadron aircraft off Yarmouth. Jock Cunningham, however, disputes this:

> I am interested to know that Marsh claims that Lawson went down 15 miles off the Dutch coast. It would be interesting to know at what altitude as I did not see any enemy fighters at mast-height – the altitude at which we were flying. I missed Lawson about six-eight miles inland on the way in.

From records, Pilot Officer Marsh was certainly the last person to see Squadron Leader Lawson alive, which was after leaving the Dutch coast. By that time it is assumed that the Spitfires had climbed to a more appropriate altitude, which is when the Me 109s attacked, having a more suitable opportunity for an ambush than among the maelstrom of aircraft at zero feet over Rotterdam docks which was in any case a hotbed of flak which knew neither friend from foe. Or was it just a question of yet again the speed of combat deceiving the human eye – and if so whose ? Whatever happened, Squadron Leader Lawson DFC remains missing to this day. Jock Cunningham recalls:

During the 100 mile North Sea crossing we flew so low that the Blenheim airscrews made a furrow on the sea's surface. Our height was held down so that we did not show up on the German radar. 19 Squadron with Squadron Leader Lawson leading crossed the coast south of Rotterdam and continued flying east for a few miles. The Blenheims turned more sharply after crossing the coast and went for their targets in the harbour. By this time we had turned 180° and flew down the estuary just above the Blenheims' height. There was no sign of any German aircraft and in any case we were too low to be useful in that respect. We continued drawing fire, however, from the naval vessels in the harbour. I was hit by a multiple pom-pom and started streaming glycol. My No 2 called 'Jock, you're on fire, better climb.' I started to do so but the engine began labouring. I could not gain enough height to bale out so I made for the beaches south of Amsterdam. I crash-landed on the sand – in front of a gun post. A machine-gun there fired a few warning shots and two soldiers came over and took possession. My efforts to start a fire were unsuccessful. As I had descended, my No 2, Peter Stuart, a fine Canadian, said 'Cheerio, Jock – good luck.' Sadly he was killed the next day – shot down off the Dutch coast.

Flight Lieutenant Cunningham DFC's war had come to an end, shot down not in aerial combat but by AA fire. The German machine-gunners of 'Küstenposten 3 der 9 Kompanie III Battalion, Infantrie Regiment 723', were credited with having shot Jock down. That claim, however, Jock disputes:

That is horsecock! I was absolutely positive, beyond question, that the hits which knocked me down came from multiple pom-poms on a ship in the estuary. The hits ruined my engine, I became a streamer and after comment by Peter Stuart, my number two, instead of heading out to sea, I tried to gain height. As I got back to the coast (going west), my engine seized and so I turned south to make a wheels-up landing on the sand. At this stage 'Küstenposten 3 der 9 Kompanie III Battalion, Infantrie Regiment 723', fired a few machine-gun bullets at me from a post in the dunes. Then a platoon of 'goons' took over.

Now a prisoner of war, Flight Lieutenant Cunningham was taken to the Officers' Mess:

After a glass of champagne and some tomato sandwiches it started to penetrate that I was a prisoner of war, that I had survived and had a future! Such a thought had actually been excluded from my mind since the start of the war. In the Mess they had a three-piece orchestra playing 'J'attendrai' and 'Sur le pont d'Avignon', all very emotional for a shot-down airman.

After a night in a cell at Amsterdam goal I travelled with the crews of two Blenheims to Dulag Luft at Doasch near Frankfurt. This was an interrogation centre through which aircrew passed en route to less pleasant conditions. I then had nearly four years in a PoW camp. Waiting for me at the gates of Dulag Luft was Dennis Cowley, also of 19 Squadron, who greeted me with 'Your — dog!' My dog had bitten Oxlin's thumb, so he couldn't fly. Cowley was going on a 48 hour leave but took Oxlin's place. Cowley was then shot down – another little drama.

I suppose that the episode of our trip to Rotterdam at least provided a paragraph in the Daily Mirror: 'Yesterday our aircraft bombed — .'

The loss of both its CO and a flight commander hit 19 Squadron hard. Arthur Vokes found himself promoted to acting flight lieutenant and assumed temporary command of the Squadron. The following morning, he led eleven of 19 Squadron's Spitfires on a search for Squadron Leader Lawson, as the ORB relates:

East coast was crossed at 12,000 feet and the squadron proceeded on a vector of 130° from base in order to arrive in the area where our missing pilot was last seen, about 10–15 miles off the Dutch coast from the Hague. Our aircraft swept the area but without success and were just about to return home when they encountered a formation of about 10 Me 110s at about 500 feet. The enemy aircraft were in line astern and apparently engaged in bombing practice as there were smoke floats in the sea.

The Me 110s belonged to 6/ZG76 which was employed on coastal defence. The combat that followed was ferocious. Although the

Me 110s outnumbered by one aircraft, this combat must represent one of the rare occasions when the twin-engined Me 110 came off significantly best against the Spitfire: 19 Squadron lost four aircraft. Pilot Officers Stuart and Edmunds, and Davies and Parkin, were all killed. In response, the Squadron claimed the destruction of two Me 110s and two more damaged. In reality, however, only one Me 110 suffered '15%' damage. For 19 Squadron the sortie was clearly an absolute disaster; no trace of Squadron Leader Lawson was ever found.

A week later, Acting Flight Lieutenant Arthur Vokes was also killed. On 5 September 1941, the temporary CO of 19 Squadron took off on a ferry flight from Coltishall to Matlaske. Visibility was poor and the cloudbase descended dangerously low. As the pilot emerged from cloud he realized just how low he was, desperately attempted to flatten out but crashed into a field near Langham aerodrome. Undoubtedly the loss of two close friends, 'Farmer' Lawson and 'Jock' Cunningham, and the subsequent loss of four pilots on the air sea rescue sortie, had played heavily on his mind. On 2 February 1942, Flight Lieutenant Cunningham wrote to Vokes's mother from Oflag XC:

Pilot Officers Andrews, Cowley and myself, all of the same squadron send our very deepest sympathies to you and Mr Vokes. Arthur and I were together for a very long time. We were on duty together and spent our leisure time together. I don't know how I should have felt if I had been left with both Farmer gone. Arthur was always happy in what he was doing and most certainly fulfilled the greatest duty asked of him by his country.

Jock Cunningham now adds:

> With Farmer's death and accompanying losses, a period of stable
> operation ended and the Squadron, I understand, was withdrawn
> from active service for a period. Farmer Lawson had been a good
> friend to me for what was, in those days, a long time. Like Brian
> Lane, who was also killed in action and similarly reported missing
> over the North Sea, he was another very competent and respected
> leader. I always regretted, however, that my departure from the
> scene had not been on a more worthwhile project.

This story brings sharply into focus the uncertainties of a fighter
pilot's wartime existence. Surviving some great campaign or
battle, such as that fought over England in summer 1940, was no
guarantee of long-term survival. After the Battle of Britain, many
survivors were killed in action or on incidents on active service,
such as flying accidents, or, like Wallace Cunningham, captured
by the enemy. Others were physically maimed while the scars of
some were psychological. The same, of course, could be said of
servicemen in any of the armed forces, which brings us back to
the beginning: it is the collective effort and experience that was
important, and the stories of those involved – the 'also rans' – must
not be forgotten.

ACKNOWLEDGEMENTS

I would like to thank all of the Few who have so kindly put themselves at my disposal over the years, revisiting memories that were not always happy ones. This book was really the idea of my publisher, Jonathan Reeve at Amberley, whose enthusiasm is always a tonic.

ILLUSTRATION CREDITS:

All images are © Dilip Sarkar.

SELECT BIBLIOGRAPHY

Primary unpublished sources:

Correspondence and interviews with the Few, Dilip Sarkar Archive

Pilots' flying log books:

Group Captain Sir D.R.S. Bader (RAF Museum)

Wing Commander B.J. Jennings

Squadron Leader B.J.E. Lane (National Archive)

Squadron Leader W.J. Lawson (National Archive)

Squadron Leader P.C. Pinkham

Flight Lieutenant A.F. Vokes

Wing Commander G.C. Unwin

Operations Record Books (all in AIR 27 at the National Archive, Kew):

Fighter squadrons: 19, 56, 151, 213, 222, 238, 242, 257, 310, 501, 603, 607 & 616.

The Combat Reports for the fighter squadrons listed above were invaluable, all in AIR 50 at the National Archive.

Published sources:

Bekker, Cajus, *The Luftwaffe War Diaries*, MacDonald & Co Ltd, 1966

Ellan, Sqn Ldr B.J., *Spitfire! The Experiences of a Fighter Pilot*, John Murray, 1942

Foreman, J., *RAF Fighter Command Victory Claims of World War Two, Part One: 1939–40*, Red Kite, 2003

Franks, N., *RAF Fighter Command Losses of the Second World War, Volume One, Operational Losses: Aircraft & Crews, 1939–41*, Midland Publishing 1997

Jefford, Wg Cdr A., *RAF Squadrons*, Airlife, 1988

Mason, F.K., *Battle Over Britain*, Aston Publications, 1990

Overy, R., *The Battle*, Penguin, 2000

Price, Dr A., *Battle of Britain Day: 15 September 1940*, Sidgwick & Jackson, 1990

Ramsey, W. (ed), *The Battle of Britain: Then & Now, Mk V*, Battle of Britain Prints International, 1989

Ramsey, W. (ed), *The Blitz Then & Now, Volume One*, Battle of Britain Prints International Ltd, 1987

Ramsey, W. (ed), *The Blitz Then & Now, Volume Two*, Battle of Britain Prints International Ltd, 1988

Sarkar, D., *Spitfire Squadron: No 19 Squadron at War, 1939–41*, Air Research Publications, 1990

Sarkar, D., *The Invisible Thread: A Spitfire's Tale*, Ramrod, 1992

Sarkar, D., *Through Peril to the Stars: RAF Fighter Pilots Who Failed to Return 1939–45*, Ramrod 1993

Sarkar, D., *Angriff Westland: Three Battle of Britain Air Raids Through the Looking Glass*, Ramrod, 1994

Sarkar, D., *A Few of the Many: Air War 1939–45, a Kaleidoscope of Memories*, Ramrod, 1995

Sarkar, D., *Bader's Duxford Fighters: The Big Wing Controversy*, Ramrod, 1997

Sarkar, D., *Missing in Action: Resting in Peace?*, Ramrod, 1998

Sarkar, D., *Battle of Britain: Last Look Back*, Ramrod, 2001

Sarkar, D., *Spitfire! Courage & Sacrifice*, Victory Books, 2006

Sarkar, D., *Duxford 1940: A Battle of Britain Base at War*, Amberley, 2009

Wynn, K.G., *Men of the Battle of Britain*, Gliddon Books, 1989

Available from February 2010 from Amberley Publishing

WAR OFFICE

SPITFIRE
MANUAL
1940

How to fly the legendary fighter plane in combat using the manuals and instructions supplied by the RAF during the Second World War

An amazing array of leaflets, books and manuals were issued by the War Office during the Second World War to aid pilots in flying the Supermarine Spitfire, here for the first time they are collated into a single book with the original 1940s setting. An introduction is supplied by expert aviation historian Dilip Sarkar. Other sections include aircraft recognition, how to act as an RAF officer, bailing out etc.

£9.99 Paperback
40 illustrations
264 pages
978-1-84868-436-2

Available from all good bookshops or to order direct
please call **01285-760-030**
www.amberley-books.com

Available from April 2010 from Amberley Publishing

BARRY SUTTON

Fighter Boy

Life as a Battle of Britain Pilot

The Battle of Britain memoir of Hurricane pilot Barry Sutton, DFC

At 23 years of age, Barry Sutton had experienced more than the average person experiences in a lifetime. This book, based on a diary he kept during the war, covers September 1939 to September 1940 when he was shot down and badly burned.

£20 Hardback
20 illustrations
224 pages
978-1-84868-849-0

Available from April 2010 from all good bookshops or to order direct please call **01285-760-030**
www.amberley-books.com

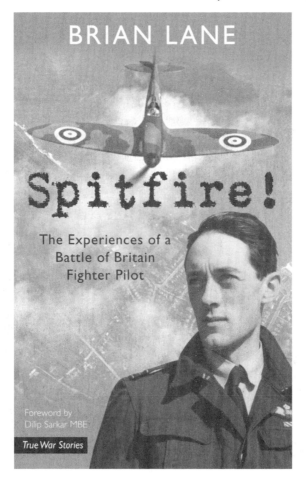

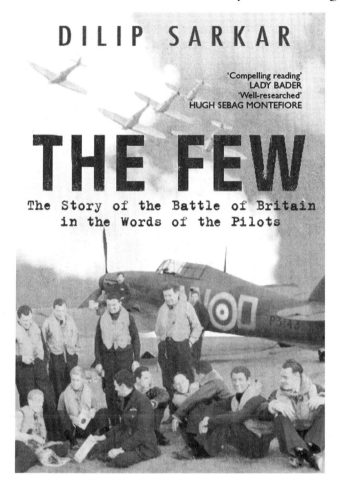